Advance Praise for
Who's Going to Run General Motors?

From Corporate Leaders and Business Consultants

"An excellent book. . . . Green and Seymour argue persuasively that America's corporations need a generation of young people who can communicate well, think, reason, solve problems, and lead in a global economy. I agree wholeheartedly."

> —David Kearns
> Chairman, Xerox Corporation

"With pinpoint accuracy describes how college students today can acquire the twenty-first-century skills needed for business success tomorrow."

> —Michael D. Moser
> Vice President, Tiffany & Co.

"An excellent resource for helping students make the transition from the world of academic theory to the reality of today's global work environment."

> —Gale Varma
> Recruiting Manager, AT&T

"Green and Seymour have penned a 'must-read' book for anyone interested in maximizing a business curriculum. Who's Going to Run General Motors? poses insightful questions to those students intent on becoming the doers of the twenty-first century."

> —Roy Huebner
> Director, Studio Operations
> The Walt Disney Studios

"An excellent guide for attaining the knowledge that previously came only through experience."

> —Jody Krall, Director of Sales
> Center for Corporate Health, Inc.
> A Subsidiary of the Travelers
> Insurance Companies

"Must reading for aware students, responsible parents, and forward-thinking human resource professionals."

—J. Anthony Burnham, Esq.
Executive Vice President
Quest Consulting
Former Vice President, Human
Resources
Carnation Company

"Highlights learning outcomes that are clearly needed for success in any organization in the twenty-first century. Both students and educators should take the message of this book seriously."

—Jeffrey H. Hallet, Management
Consultant and Founder
The PresentFutures Group

"A practical guide for today's student focused on the next century's economy. The authors identify important skills and translate them into actual course offerings or campus activities."

—Kent H. Hughes
President, Council on
Competitiveness

From Academia

"Useful for all college students thinking about a career in business, no matter what academic major they plan to pursue."

—Peter Likins
President, Lehigh University

"Green and Seymour offer important, practical advice about career planning and professional development. Who's Going to Run General Motors? should be required reading for undergraduate business students."

—Jon P. Goodman, Director,
Entrepreneur Program
School of Business Administration
University of Southern California

Who's Going to Run General Motors?

What College Students Need to Learn Today to Become the Business Leaders of Tomorrow

Kenneth C. Green, Ph.D.
University of Southern California

Daniel T. Seymour, Ph.D.
KPMG Peat Marwick

Peterson's Guides
Princeton, New Jersey

Library of Congress Cataloging-in-Publication Data

Green, Kenneth C.
    Who's going to run General Motors? : what college
students need to learn today to become the business leaders
of tomorrow / Kenneth C. Green, Daniel T. Seymour.
        p.   cm.
    ISBN 1-56079-037-7
    1. Business education—United States. 2. Management—
Study and teaching—United States. 3. College student
orientation—United States. 4. Vocational guidance—United
States. I. Seymour, Daniel T. II. Title.
HF1131.G725   1991
650'.071'173—dc20   90-49064

Composition and design by Peterson's Guides

Cover design by Molly Eklund-Huhn

Printed in the United States of America

10 9 8 7 6 5 4 3 2 1

*To Aaron and Mara
and to Ray and Kate Seymour.*

Contents

Preface

The last years of the twentieth century will be a period of rapid change. Political, social, economic, scientific, and technological change will occur quickly and frequently throughout your adult life, at a pace far faster than the rate of change that either your parents or grandparents experienced. We only have to look at events in the closing years of the 1980s to understand just how quickly—and unexpectedly—dramatic change can occur.

- The closing months of 1989 saw the fall of the Berlin Wall and dramatic changes in the political structure of Eastern Europe. These fantastic events—in Germany, Hungary, Poland, and Romania—caught most Western governments completely by surprise. Many government analysts had expected the Iron Curtain, which has divided Eastern and Western Europe since the end of World War II, to last for another twenty-five or even fifty years.

- Throughout the 1980s, computers changed the way many people learn, work, and think about information. When IBM introduced its "PC" in 1981, it never expected to sell more than 100,000 systems over the life of the product. Three years later, IBM was selling 100,000 PC systems *each month*. Today, inexpensive desktop computers—far more powerful than the room-sized machines of the sixties and seventies—are common in schools, businesses, and homes. People who are not computer programmers have found that they can be, nonetheless, very sophisticated computer users.

- As recently as twenty years ago, Japanese products had a reputation for being cheap and shoddy. In the mid-1970s, many Americans laughed when they heard that Honda, until then best known as a manufacturer of inexpensive motorcycles, would export cars to the United States. Today, Japanese goods are often perceived to be better designed and manufactured than competitive American products. Japan is a world leader in computer chips and electronics. And one Honda product, the Acura, has ranked at the top of consumer satisfaction surveys for the past three years.

- In 1992, the twelve nations of the European Economic Community (the Common Market) will merge into an economic, political, and monetary union that will change the face of Europe and the course of European history. Nations and cultures that have competed with each other—politically, economically, and militarily—for more than a thousand years will voluntarily merge into a single, and generally borderless, continent-sized nation-state.

In short, we only have to look around to see that change will be the only constant in our lives during the 1990s and twenty-first century.

This book is about preparing for a changing world. We wrote *Who's Going to Run General Motors?* as a guide for today's college students and tomorrow's business professionals. It will not help you choose a major, prepare a resume, or develop a job search strategy. Rather, this book is a guide—intended to help you get the most out of your college experience and to help you prepare for the ever-changing world you will encounter after you leave college.

How will we do it? Think for a moment about an artist who is interviewing for a job. The artist brings along a portfolio—examples of his or her work that demonstrate specific artistic skills, insights, and vision. Artists are always expanding and enhancing their portfolios; they are eager to include new material that reveals new skills or a special sense of color or mood. *Who's Going to Run General Motors?* will help you develop a portfolio of fundamental skills that will help you succeed in the business world of the twenty-first century.

Now think about your portfolio. Without question you will acquire some very important skills in your college classes: a basic understanding of accounting, finance, marketing, and so on. But these are *technical* skills, subject to change and obsolescence. For example, your technical knowledge of accounting may quickly become obsolete if changes in the tax code affect key practices relating to amortization schedules and investment credits. (This actually happened to thousands of accountants following major changes in the tax code in 1982 and again in 1987.)

Who's Going to Run General Motors? focuses on *fundamental* skills—the infrastructure of your portfolio—that will help you throughout your working years after college. We identify the seven fundamental skills that every college student—every future business professional—should acquire. We explain why these skills are important in the business world of the 1990s and the twenty-first century. We also identify ways in which you can develop these skills as part of your college experience.

Why are these seven skills important? Because American businesses—both large corporations and small firms—are desperately seeking new employees with these talents to help them as they confront increasing competition at home and from abroad.

In sum, *Who's Going to Run General Motors?* is about *changes* and *choices:* changes you *should* make in the way you approach your college experience and choices you *can* make while you are in college to help you prepare for your future as a business professional in the twenty-first century.

Kenneth C. Green   Daniel T. Seymour
Encino, California   Los Angeles, California
October 1990   October 1990

Acknowledgments

Chapter 7 of this book emphasizes the importance of teamwork. We want to acknowledge the team of people who helped us as this book moved from a concept to an outline, on through several draft manuscripts and into the published product.

A number of business executives and college faculty members were very generous with their time. In particular, our conversations with Rhonda Beran (director of marketing at Computer Resources Group), Anthony Burnham (executive vice president at Quest Consulting), and Bernard Hargadon (president, McKesson International) were especially informative, providing key insights into the skills that corporations seek in their newly hired employees. On the academic side, conversations with Jon Goodman (director of the Entrepreneur Program at USC), Gene Warren (management science professor at Chapman College), and Lyman Porter (former dean of the business program at the University of California, Irvine) increased our understanding of some of the challenges confronting both business programs and business students in the 1990s.

We greatly appreciate the interest and efforts of several people at Peterson's Guides. Jim Gish, our editor, and Wayne Anderson, vice president of Peterson's Publishing Group, worked with us as we converted an interesting idea into what we hope is a useful book. Jim, in particular, offered important feedback and direction at key milestones in the development of the manuscript. Larry Wexler and Susan Dilts deftly and patiently guided this manuscript through the final editing and production stages. We also thank Peter and Casey Hegener, president and executive vice president, respectively, of Peterson's Guides, for their personal interest in and continuing support for this project.

Finally—and closer to home—we owe a major debt to family and close friends who suffered through the late nights, long hours, and often frantic, often erratic work schedule that became part of this book experience. In the Green household, son Aaron, daughter Mara, and wife Rika were very supportive, often sacrificing weekend time for us to work on the book. Necessary diversions to the Seymour work ethic were provided by Ray, Sandahl, Margit, Evan, Steve, Chris, and, of course, Stunzi.

I

The
Context

1

A World Turned
Upside Down

Ross Perot, the self-made American billionaire, is concerned about the future of the United States: "When I go to Asia or Europe I feel like I'm looking at tomorrow. When I go to many U.S. cities, I see decay and neglect and I feel like I'm looking at yesterday. The only way to bulletproof our country is to design and make the best products in the world."

Who will respond to this challenge? Who will lead the way?

Will it be Ross Perot, Lee Iacocca, or other senior executives in U.S. companies? The answer is yes—and no. The rejuvenation of the U.S. economy requires change. Industry leaders can sound the trumpets and beat the drums. And many of them are doing just that. In the recent sixtieth-anniversary issue of *Fortune* magazine, over 100 business leaders, professors, and economists reflected on "an American vision for the 1990s." Here's what some of these leaders have to say about the future.

> The pace of change in the nineties will make the eighties look like a picnic—a walk in the park. Competition will be relentless. The bar of excellence in everything we do will be raised every day.
> John F. Welch Jr., CEO, General Electric

> When you contemplate the future of the computer industry, I think it raises another question: Will there even be a U.S. computer industry ten years from now? I'd say the odds are only fifty-fifty.
> Steve Jobs, president and CEO, NeXT Inc.

> In the 1990s we will reinvent management—and constantly modify our invention. I expect all varieties of participative management and em-

ployee involvement to spread, partly because the traditional systems of managing are failing.

Edward E. Lawler III, professor,
University of Southern California

I'm sorry that I'm not younger! The nineties are going to be so unbelievably great for alert manufacturers, merchants, [and] service companies. Vision is now a key word: Retailers and manufacturers who don't have it are just not going to make it.

Charles Lazarus, CEO, Toys "R" Us

American business has got to perform differently in the 1990s. We can't sit around and commiserate with one another—we've got to get good, we've got to compete, we've got to be world-class. We can't just shout about it, we've got to be it.

Lee Iacocca, chairman and CEO, Chrysler Corporation

Let's also consider the perspectives of several top management experts, individuals to whom corporations and small businesses turn for advice and direction.

Old ways of thinking, old formulas, dogmas, and ideologies, no matter how cherished or how useful in the past, no longer fit the facts. The world that is fast emerging from the clash of new values and technologies, new geopolitical relationships, new life-styles and modes of communication, demands wholly new ideas and analogies, classifications, and concepts. We cannot cram the embryonic world of tomorrow into yesterday's conventional cubbyholes. Nor are the orthodox attitudes or moods appropriate [for the future].

Futurist and *Third Wave* author Alvin Toffler

Self-management is replacing staff managers who manage people; the computer is replacing line managers who manage systems. . . . Corporations will aggressively compete for fewer first-rate employees. The most talented people will be attracted to those corporations that succeed in reinventing [the organization and the organizational culture] into companies that are great places to work . . . because the people in [these firms] grow personally while contributing to the company.

Futurists John Naisbitt and Patricia Aburdene, authors
of *Reinventing the Corporation*

Successful organizations today are those which are adapting their current organizational behavior to the realities of the current environment. That environment is one of constant, unyielding change as we surge into the Information Age. Nothing is secure for the next 20 years. . . . Survival and success depend on innovation, creativity, and flexibility. . . . Today's new models of worklife are teams, work groups, quality circles, task forces, etc., assembled from among those [people] within the organization whose mix of skills and experience— regardless of their previous position or place—best meet the current challenges. (Original emphasis.)

Management consultant Jeffrey Hallett

We are talking about a world turned upside down. The old ways are out. New is in. *New* management systems. *New* ways to compete. *New* visions. *New* ways to motivate employees. But the necessary changes cannot be mandated from above. None of these business leaders—not the Lee Iacoccas, Ross Perots, or John Welches of the U.S. business establishment—can impose the necessary changes from their offices at the top of the corporate structure. The much-needed bold departure from past behavior and corporate practices will require an effort by *everyone* in U.S. business organizations, in large corporations and small firms alike. Hourly employees, midlevel management, newly hired management trainees, technical professionals, and support staff *must all see* their future as being closely intertwined with their company's success.

And what about you? What's your role in all this?

The twenty-first century is less than ten years away. Many of today's college students—you, your friends, and your peers—will not yet be *thirtysomething* when the year 2001 rolls around. You will just have begun your working life. You will be in the early stages of a career that will extend for the next forty or fifty years, until 2040 or 2050.

This world turned upside down, then, is your world just as much as it is that of Steve Jobs or John Welch. How can we bulletproof business professionals and U.S. businesses in this new world? There is only one sure way. Today's students (tomorrow's business professionals) must understand tomorrow's business challenges and what it will take to be competitive and successful in the rapidly changing world of business and commerce. You cannot wait to learn about these things until you begin your first job after college. *Tomorrow will be too late.* So you need to learn to work smart, beginning today and for the rest of the time you are in college. As a future business professional, you need to bulletproof yourself against this topsy-turvy world.

That's exactly what this book is all about. This book is about the future, about the skills that tomorrow's business professionals will need to be successful in a rapidly changing world. It is about making the most of your college experience in preparation for the career challenges of the 1990s and the twenty-first century.

So let's begin by exploring two questions that will be an important part of your life for the next few years: "What's your major?" and "Why should we hire you?" The first question is a *campus* question: It is about your experience in college. The second one, in contrast, is a *career* question: It is central to a job interview. How you answer these questions, not just in conversation but by making choices about classes and by acquiring key experiences and skills, will go a long way toward determining your future success.

What's Your Major?

The most commonly asked question on a college campus today is "What's your major?" It shows up on all the forms and records that you fill out. It is also the second question asked at any social gathering, right after "What's your name?" Many students (and their parents) believe that an undergraduate business major offers the best preparation for a career in business. The appeal of a business degree seems fairly obvious today, yet this strong interest in business majors and business careers marks a real change in undergraduate career preferences over the past two decades. College campuses—and college students—have changed dramatically in twenty years.

Back in the 1960s there was some real campus snobbery about the liberal arts. Students were interested in *relevance*. They wanted to study subjects that would help them make sense of the world. A profit-and-loss statement was boring compared with the complexities of the Russian Revolution, a Robert Frost poem, or a scheme to change the world. The thought of becoming a merchant or corporation man (there were few corporation women back then!) was alien to the sixties culture, which viewed big business with disdain. Thinking great thoughts (or thinking it was possible to think great thoughts) was more stimulating (and more esteemed) than thinking about ways to market cigarettes, candy, or cars. Besides, the economy was healthy; almost everyone enrolled in college seemed fairly confident of finding a good job after graduation. Consequently, comparatively few students focused on long-term career planning.

Oh, yes, occasionally you found someone who would admit to being an accounting or management major. But these folks were vastly outnumbered by the legions of liberal arts students—history, political science, philosophy, English, psychology, and biology majors.

How things have changed over two decades! Business and management accounted for roughly 250,000 (over 25 percent) of the 990,000 undergraduate degrees awarded in 1989; this compares with just 14 percent—some 114,000 business and management degrees—of the total 839,000 undergraduate degrees awarded in 1971. Today, the

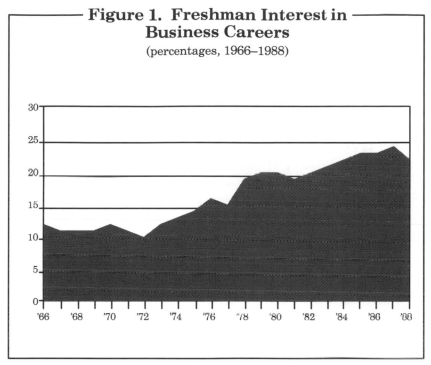

Figure 1. Freshman Interest in Business Careers

(percentages, 1966–1988)

Source: Alexander W. Astin, Kenneth C. Green, William S. Korn, Marilynn Schalit, and Ellyne R. Berz, *The American Freshman: National Norms for Fall 1988* (Higher Education Research Institute, University of California, Los Angeles), 1988.

growth has stabilized such that nearly one out of every four freshmen entering college plans to major in business, compared with just over 10 percent in the late sixties and early seventies. (See Fig. 1.)

Colleges and universities responded to the rising demand for business programs by expanding their business and management programs. They hired more faculty, brought computers into the classroom, and broadened the scope of their programs to include the management of nonprofit organizations and international trade. Even the die-hard liberal arts colleges, where some faculty members view business as an "evil" influence, acknowledged changing student interests. These campuses developed new academic programs in marketing, management, accounting, and finance. At many campuses, the business school now seems like an efficient factory running on overtime and double shifts, turning out large numbers of tomorrow's businessmen and businesswomen. (See Table 1.)

What fueled the strong student interest in business? The growing attractiveness of a business degree was linked to several factors.

Table 1. The Largest U.S. Business Schools, by Enrollment

(total enrollment, full-time and part-time students)

1.	Baruch College, City University of New York	12,030
2.	Arizona State University	8,908
3.	University of Texas at Austin	8,733
4.	San Diego State University	7,747
5.	Northeastern University	7,656
6.	Michigan State University	7,332
7.	California State University, Fullerton	6,959
8.	Georgia State University	6,255
9.	University of Arizona	6,222
10.	Western Michigan University	6,216

Source: 1989 survey of member institutions, *American Assembly of Collegiate Schools of Business Newsline* (vol. 20, no. 3), February 1990, p. 3.

The Women's Movement

One very important factor has been the soaring interest in business majors and careers among young women. The women's movement of the 1970s altered societal expectations and broke down many employment barriers that had channeled women into traditionally female careers, such as teaching, social work, and nursing. Between 1966 and 1988 the proportion of women who entered college planning to pursue business careers increased sevenfold—from 3 percent in 1966 to 22 percent in 1988! Similarly, the number of undergraduate business degrees awarded to women soared from 15,000 in 1968 to well over 100,000 some twenty years later. Women now account for more than 40 percent of undergraduate business graduates; in some concentrations, such as accounting, women now outnumber men.

Careerism

Another factor contributing to the rising student interest in business had its roots in the changing culture of the 1970s and 1980s. The political activism and social concern of the previous decade gave way to a more self-focused concern with getting ahead. Between 1976 and 1988 the proportion of freshmen indicating that the opportunity to make more money was a very important factor in their decision to attend college rose from 53 to 73 percent. At the same time, the proportion of those who cited getting a general education as a very important factor in their decision to attend college dropped from 65 to 60 percent. (See Fig. 2.)

This shift in values has affected a number of choices. For example, surveys of high school students found that the influences on choice of a college had changed significantly. "Jobs obtained by graduates" began to challenge "the caliber of the faculty" as the primary reason for selecting one college over another. More specifically, the choice of a major was driven by a set of practical needs. In one study, in which business students were asked what factors had the greatest impact on their choice of major, the top influence was "interest in the area," followed by "job security" and "financial rewards."

And finally, there is little doubt that the economic costs and benefits of attending college have been a factor in the rising student interest in business. Academics and other intellectuals have always looked at the outcomes of college in ideal terms—intellectual and emotional development, a learned society involved in civic activities, and so forth. But as the cost of college has grown, students are asking a more direct question: Is college a good investment? Until the 1970s, the answer to this question was uniformly affirmative; college graduates could expect to earn far more than their contemporaries without a degree working in almost any area. In the mid-1970s, however, as

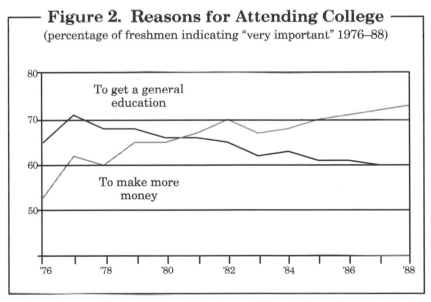

Figure 2. Reasons for Attending College

(percentage of freshmen indicating "very important" 1976–88)

To get a general education

To make more money

'76   '78   '80   '82   '84   '86   '88

Source: Alexander W. Astin, Kenneth C. Green, William S. Korn, Marilynn Schalit, and Ellyne R. Berz, *The American Freshman: National Norms for Fall 1988* (Higher Education Research Institute, University of California, Los Angeles), 1988.

large numbers of baby-boom students entered the market, job opportunities for college graduates declined. The earnings differential dropped: Plumbers made more money than schoolteachers, and tens of thousands of trained teachers could not find a classroom job. Given rising costs and the apparent decline in economic returns, students and their parents have begun to look very closely at the economic investment of going to college. Does a degree enable a student to get a better job? To make more money? To get ahead faster? These questions reflect legitimate concerns. College *is* expensive; indeed, it is the third most expensive investment U.S. families will make, after purchasing a home and buying cars. Moreover, the cost of college continues to rise: Whereas median family income increased by only 6 percent between 1970 and 1986, the cost of attending an independent university jumped by one third, and the cost of attending a public university increased by more than one fifth.

In the face of increasing costs, many people have made the logical connection between the costs of a college degree and the prospects for future employment. The trick, according to them, is to get marketable skills, to translate the degree into a good job that pays real dollars. Political science and psychology are interesting enough, but they don't "impact the bottom line." In fact, some have questioned whether

"ISN'T IT TIME YOU WERE ENTERING YOUR CHOSEN FIELD?"

it is really possible to get anywhere in the job market with a liberal arts degree.

Many students and their parents believe that college simply costs too much today to spend time on such "irrelevant" courses as Greek philosophy, medieval European history, and the structure of the Victorian theater. They believe a practical major is what will be important and affect job opportunities. They feel that they don't have time to "waste" on anything that isn't *marketable*. (Later we'll see that what is practical and marketable must be redefined in terms of ongoing changes and developments in the business world.)

Is this the answer then? Just get a business degree and you'll be set for the world described by Lee Iacocca, Ross Perot, and the others a few pages back? Let's hold off answering that question for a few more pages. First, we need to look at our second question.

Why Should We Hire You?

While college campuses were changing, the companies that hire college graduates were also changing. Indeed, the entire corporate environment in this country was and still is undergoing a radical transformation. For example, our "Age" has come to be called the Information Age. We see the reason all around us, from the number of choices we have on cable television to the nutritional information on cereal boxes. We used to have one Yellow Pages. Now we have a dozen. This hot commodity—*information*—has also become part of the corporate environment. John Naisbitt and Patricia Aburdene, in their bestselling book, *Reinventing the Corporation*, discuss the shift to information as a strategic corporate resource. They see growing value placed on information, knowledge, and creativity—and on the people who can supply these things.

One legacy of the Industrial Age, however, is a multitiered corporate hierarchy that was designed to bring accountability to the manufacturing process. Structures and management systems were developed to control quality in the workplace. A few people, usually no more than ten, reported to a superior. That person, along with others, reported to a more superior superior. The result was a huge bureaucracy with layer upon layer of midlevel managers whose job it was to see that their ten subordinates were working hard.

But this turn-of-the-century mentality is being challenged in the Information Age. James O'Toole, professor of corporate strategy at the University of Southern California, has studied span of control—the number of people a person has reporting to him or her. While U.S. firms average one supervisor to ten nonsupervisors, the Japanese ratio can run one to a hundred. Not surprisingly, he concludes: "In general, American workers appear to be oversupervised." Another recent study of forty-one large companies by A. T. Kearney, a Chicago-based management consultant firm, contrasted winning and losing companies on the basis of long-term profitability. The winners had 3.9 fewer layers of management than the losers (7.2 versus 11.1).

The conclusion is that the Information Age requires the horizontal coordination of information, not the vertical control of people. We don't need more managers checking on people; we need fewer yet more effective managers. As U.S. firms begin to discover how bloated they have become, they also are beginning to make the inevitable (and absolutely necessary) reductions and reorganizations. For example:

- Brunswick Corporation recently reduced management by 40 percent. The cuts involved mostly senior executives. Initial expectations that this would result in overworked middle-managers never materialized. In fact, Brunswick was able to make substantial cuts at the middle level as well, once it became obvious that staff had been spending the majority of their time responding to requests flowing down from the upper-level managers.

- The transformation of IBM has been extensive. Walton Burdick, director of IBM's worldwide personnel organization, recently commented: "We set out to reduce the number of people we had in the company and to change the skill mix of our people. We needed to move a significant number from overhead skills to areas that were either producing revenue directly or developing products or programs that would." Between 1985 and 1988, IBM trimmed staff by 16,000 and shifted another 21,000 employees into high-priority business areas, moving office-based managers into the field to work directly with clients. Late in 1989 IBM announced plans to trim another 10,000 people from its payroll.

- The *Wall Street Journal,* the extraordinarily successful and popular daily newspaper for business executives, saw paid circulation slip from a peak of 2.11 million in 1983 to 1.95 million in 1988. The 1987–88 plunge of 8 percent was blamed partly on the "decline in management ranks at many corporations."

Today, downsizing is a national fact of life. And 80 percent of the U.S. firms that employ 5,000 or more workers have reduced their work force in the past four years.

Downsizing at McDonnell Douglas

According to Robert H. Hood Jr., the new president of the aircraft manufacturing firm McDonnell Douglas, the company is beset by inadequate quality on its production lines, antiquated management systems, high costs, disorderly procedures, a messy factory, and looming future losses if conditions don't change. One of the key factors underlying these conditions, according to Hood, is that getting communications from top management down the line takes too long, part of a pattern he says has existed since McDonnell bought Douglas in 1967.

Under direction from McDonnell Douglas chairman John F. McDonnell, a top-to-bottom overhaul of Douglas began in 1989. The procedure being employed is called the Total Quality Management System (TQMS), and its goal is a 15 percent reduction in the number of hours it takes to build an aircraft. One of the keys will be the elimination of several layers of management. According to Stefan Schurter, a senior engineering designer, the commitment is serious: "We thought that the restructuring would only affect the 'little people.' But one of the first things they did was to eliminate the executive vice president's position and half of the 20 vice presidents. The total number of management levels went from seven to five, from 5,000 people to 4,000. The other change that is making a tremendous difference is that, before, a good engineer had to become a supervisor to make more money. The new organization chart has as many levels of technical specialists as managers—and with the same pay scale. It's great. We are getting recognized for our ability, and we don't need an M.B.A. to advance in the company."

How about another transformation? Even as the nation's largest firms are trimming their payrolls, total employment in the United States has *increased* by 9 million jobs. Fortune 500 companies alone shrank by some 3 million jobs between 1980 and 1987, the equivalent of laying off the entire work force, public and private, of the state of Massachusetts. How can this be? How can the country's largest firms drop 3 million workers yet total employment expand by some 9 million jobs, even *after* cuts at the Fortune 500 firms? This little-known phenomenon is due to the huge increase in the "hidden economy," the tens of thousands of smaller, private firms that attract minimal attention.

How important is this hidden economy? The United States has gone from 93,000 new incorporations in 1950 to around 700,000 in

1988. Most of these new companies, 85 or 90 percent, have 100 or fewer employees when they start their growth. MIT professor David Birch refers to this process as the "atomization of the economy": The business of the United States is now being done by a larger and larger number of firms that are smaller and smaller in size. These companies, because of their size, must be innovative in finding and exploiting niches in the marketplace. They are not going to overwhelm anyone with their human or capital resources, nor are they going to scare General Electric or General Mills with their product line. They compete by their wits, not by brute strength, by finding specific opportunities and then creatively satisfying a need. They are quick, flexible, and innovative.

Another transformation? While the workplace has never been the exclusive domain of native-born white men, the population of corporate America is more diverse than ever before. "The graduates of today have a much greater probability of working with or for people who are not like themselves," says Roosevelt Thomas, president of the American Institute for Managing Diversity, an independent affiliate of Morehouse College in Atlanta. Over the next ten years, only 15 percent of new U.S. workers will be native-born white males, according to the Hudson Institute, a New York think tank. The U.S. Bureau of Labor Statistics is in full agreement, predicting that in the next decade the number of white males in the work force will increase by only 9 percent, compared with 22 percent for white women, 29 percent for blacks, 71 percent for Asians, and 74 percent for Hispanics.

One final example: Not only has the world turned upside down, but it has also shrunk. Picture a typical U.S. college student—driving a Japanese car and listening to Japanese audio equipment, sporting Korean-made athletic shoes, and wearing Levis or designer jeans assembled in either Mexico or the Far East. What about the typical U.S. consumer: outfitted with a Swiss-made Swatch watch, a Japanese Minolta camera, an Ivy-League-styled shirt made in Hong Kong, and Italian shoes and drinking Colombian coffee. In short, Americans import a broad range of foreign goods. Moreover, there is even reason to doubt the extent to which some of our American products are homegrown. There is ample evidence of the growth of international cooperation in the design, production, and distribution of an increasing number of products. For example, Ford workers assemble cars in Mexico in a plant jointly owned by Mazda and Ford, using parts manufactured at a Mazda plant in Japan.

Thirty percent of U.S. manufacturers today know that three of their top five competitors for the U.S. market are foreign firms. And according to Fred Steingraber, CEO of A. T. Kearney, "that [30 per-

Facts About a Growing Global Interdependence

- In recent years, four out of five new jobs in manufacturing have been created as a direct result of foreign trade.
- About one third of all U.S. corporate profits come from international activities.
- American companies have doubled their rate of investment overseas in recent years, jumping from an annual rate of $11 billion in 1986 to $22 billion in 1987, in spite of the depreciating value of the U.S. dollar.
- About one third of U.S. farmland produces products for export.
- The thirteen largest U.S. banks derive almost half of their total earnings from overseas credits.
- Fully 25 percent of the U.S. economy relies on our ability to export or import raw materials.

Source: Ralph Smuckler and Lawrence Sommers, "Internationalizing the Curriculum," *Phi Kappa Phi Journal,* Fall 1988, p. 9.

cent] is going to grow to about 45 percent in the next five years." In contrast, as recently as 1982 something less than 5 percent of U.S. manufacturers counted a single foreign firm among their five primary competitors for the U.S. market. In an age of instant communications and rapid transportation, we have to accept the fact that we now live in a global community. There is no denying a world of increasing interdependence.

It seems obvious that the answer to the question "Why should we hire you?" is much different today, and will be in the future, from what it was in the past. As American and foreign corporations scramble for position in the global marketplace, they are discovering that the organizational structures and management practices that they have lived by for decades no longer work. New challenges are creating new problems that require a different concept of the business organization. The business environment of the 1990s will require that companies be more flexible than in the past, capable of responding quickly to a fast-changing world with a lean management team—a flattened pyramidal structure. Product innovation will be important. The successful coordination of information will be important. The ability to create unique products targeted at smaller, more selective groups of consumers in an international market will be important. A new employee skills mix is required to meet these challenges.

A good summary contrasting the past and future orientation of U.S. management and predicting how this topsy-turvy world will influence the skills mix of U.S. managers has been offered by Anthony Burnham, the former vice president for human resources at Carnation Company and now a partner in Quest Consulting, a management consulting and human resources firm based in Orange County, California.

Management Contrasts

Past	Future
Domestic	Global
Short-term	Long-term
Directive	Participative
Bottom-line	Balanced results
Information "taker"	Information "giver"
Closed	Open
Top-down	Bottom-up
Authority	Competence
Static	Changing
Rigid	Flexible
Cynical	Trusting
Order	Structured chaos
Ass-kicker	Praiser
"Pusher"	"Puller"
What's wrong	What's right
Cold/detached	Warm/involved
Black/white	Gray
Uniformity	Diversity
Rules	Ethics
"Work"	"Fun"

Source: Anthony Burnham, Quest Consulting.

May We Have the Envelope, Please?

We are now prepared to give you some answers. The dilemma for today's college student is simple and straightforward. Do U.S. businesses want more of the same, more business majors? Considering that we graduate a quarter million business students each year, will there be room for one more? And will the standard business administration major be right for you and attractive to future employers? *We say most businesses don't want more of the same.* In fact, the student who just sits in the back of business classes for four years and then expects to be scooped up by major U.S. companies is in for a rude surprise.

Itel Containers International Corporation

Itel Containers International Corporation is the world's largest lessor of oceangoing containers, the giant metal crates that are used to ship products. Itel Corporation, the parent company, also owns seven small railroads and eight railcar maintenance facilities in the United States and Canada and has a huge fleet of railcars that it leases to other railroad companies. These businesses, combined with several others, created revenues of $1.6 billion in 1988 for Itel Corporation. Itel chairman Samuel Zell refers to the company as "an opportunity in transition." Growth has been nothing short of phenomenal as Itel worked to become a world-class company. And as Zell points out, its success is based upon a talented and nontraditional group of employees who helped to create a dynamic and exciting company with a great future: "Perhaps most important, we benefited from the freedom to 'make it up as we go along,' rather than focus our efforts on a business school curriculum of 'how to do it.' Superior achievements are not obtained by accepting 'conventional wisdom.'"

Such ideas are not merely the stuff of speeches. The guiding principles of Itel Containers are reflected in its hiring practices. According to Esther Lam, Itel's vice president of human resources, "We are not interested in hiring technicians, people who have managed to cram enough facts in their head to pass an accounting or management exam. The degree or even the college that a person gets it from doesn't impress me. It is the skills that they have acquired that are key to this company. We look for people who can think on their feet and are not afraid to use their intuition. They thrive on diversity and adversity. They are not worried about who gets the credit or who gets the blame, nor do they need to see which little box in the organization is theirs. We want people that dig in with a team spirit and have fun."

Source: Itel Corporation, Annual Report, 1988.

It was different in the past. A business degree would have been a sufficient answer to the question "Why should we hire you?" Now those who hire want—indeed desperately need—"new and improved" models.

If nothing else, the business major of today should become extremely familiar with the business term *differential advantage*. If there are 250,000 coffeepots being sold, why should the consumer choose yours? If there are 250,000 business graduates each year, as we have noted, why should the consumer (U.S. companies) choose you? Why?

In its early days, Ford Motor Company grew very successful by producing one car, a black Model T. Obviously, as long as the demand was strong and the competition weak, Ford could sell as many Model T's as it could produce.

Think about the Model T in the context of the future job market for college graduates. *Your product is you.* A college degree is hardly a unique commodity anymore, and a business degree is nothing very special. Consequently, your success depends on your ability to differentiate yourself from others. It depends on knowing yourself and your capabilities. Future success will depend on developing the skills that are required to be effective and perform well in a chosen field. The final key is translating those skills into specific decisions about majors, minors, courses, internships, and the broad range of experiences that are part of your college education—in the classroom, in the dorm room, and elsewhere during your college years.

This book is your guide to making these key decisions. *Let's get busy.*

The 1990s Job Market Begins with a Chill

What happens when the economy slows down and companies find themselves overstaffed? Do you think that top-level executives are asked to resign voluntarily or managers quit because they don't have enough work to keep them busy? Probably not. Instead, most companies just *freeze* their hiring. According to an annual study by researchers at Michigan State University, the 1990s have begun with a distinct chill in the air—job openings for college graduates nationwide are down 13.3 percent compared with last year. "The same student who would have had four or five offers last year is not getting any this year," says L. Patrick Scheetz, assistant director of career development and placement services at Michigan State and an author of *Recruiting Trends*.

Individual students' experiences confirm the study's findings. Georgetown University's John Doherty spent his last few months on campus checking the list of recruiters in the business school's career placement office and preparing for interviews. He also sent out dozens of letters and made scores of telephone calls. He finally landed a job as a financial analyst at Prudential-Bache Securities, Inc. "It's very tough this year," says Doherty, who graduated with a degree in finance. "I'm lucky to get something." Another frostbite victim is Timothy Bullis, who graduated from Otterbein College with a business administration degree. "I've had about ten interviews with different corporations and nothing has come of those," he says. "Right now, I'd take just about any job in business."

The Michigan State study drew responses from more than 450 employers representing business, elementary and secondary schools, government agencies, and the military services. Employers were asked about hiring trends and factors that are currently influencing the job market.

Source: Susan Dodge, "Job Market for 1990 Graduates Is the Most Competitive Since the Early 1980's, an Annual Study Finds," *The Chronicle of Higher Education*, June 13, 1990, p. A25.

2

Pieces of the Puzzle

In this world turned upside down you must plan and pursue your college education differently from the way other people, perhaps even your parents, did in the past. Not that long ago you could approach college as a safe place to be for the four or five years between graduating from high school and getting a job. The phases were distinct: high school, college, then career. While in college you decided upon a major, then took the appropriate courses to fulfill the graduation requirements. When you had accumulated enough courses, you would trade in your jeans and campus sweatshirt for a cap and gown. Next came the business suit.

The old days were great—no worries. But the old days are gone. The realities of the 1990s, summarized in Chapter 1, are here and now. And the truth is that if you want to be successful in a business career, you need to understand the secrets of success *before* you graduate from college. Why? Because in a competitive environment, victory (or the job) will not go to someone who is "willing to learn" by trial and error; it will go, instead, to the person who *has already learned* and is prepared for the challenges that lie ahead.

Let's use a silly analogy. Say you decide to go camping. You've never actually done it before, but you've heard of a great place, 4 hours away, that seems as though it would make for a nice weekend. There are two basic ways to proceed. One way would be to get in the car and start driving. Along the way you stop and pick up some items—walking shorts, a hat, a sleeping bag, some charcoal and burgers. How difficult can it be? Now you're ready for a few days with Mother Nature. The other way would be to talk to someone who is a camping enthusiast. You know this person. He or she lives and dies for weekends in the woods. Or maybe you would consult a few books on camping.

You can see where this example is going, can't you? Wouldn't you want to know the critical elements for survival in the woods *before* you got in the car and started driving? You would want to have the right equipment, rather than waste 4 hours on the road. After all, you're from the city; you don't know the woods. Burgers are great, but bug spray may be more important.

What it takes to be successful in the business world, just like camping, is not so obvious to someone who has not been there. You need to prepare for your future by knowing something about it now. When you're on the job or in the woods, it's a little too late to start learning.

Let some experts tell you about the difference between school and the "real world" of business.

> *The real world is quite different from the impression of it that a student derives from school. And unless we [help] students to realize it ahead of time, they will waste much of their talent, hard work, and enthusiasm and will erode the self-confidence that served them so well in school.*
> Paul Nadler, "Are Graduates Ready for the Real Business World?"
> *American Banker,* June 8, 1987, p. 4

And in what way does the so-called real world differ from college? What is it that students must realize as they approach the world of work? How will your future coworkers and supervisors evaluate what you know and how well you perform?

> *How effectively a manager will perform on the job cannot be predicted by the number of degrees he [or she] holds, the grades he [or she] receives in school, or the formal management education programs he [or she] attends.*
> J. Sterling Livingston, "Myth of the Well Educated Manager," quoted in Gary Benson, "Management Theory and the Practice of Management," *Journal of Business Education,* April 1985, p. 276

What factors really relate to job performance if the obvious indicators, such as grades or schooling, do not predict on-the-job effectiveness? What is the meaning of success?

> *From all this research, our most consistent finding has been that the amount of formal knowledge one acquires about a content area is generally unrelated to superior performance in an occupation. The difference between exemplary performers and typical or less-than-satisfactory performers has much more to do with how they use what they know and with certain general capacities underlying the effective use of knowledge.*
> George O. Klemp, "The Meaning of Success: A View from Outside the Academy," *Liberal Education,* May/June 1988, p. 37

The experts agree. *Success is not a necessary by-product of a college degree.* Just as being able to drive the car to the campsite is not a good indicator of success in the woods, deciding upon a major and going to classes does not guarantee you anything in the business world. Something else is required. That something else is *skills*—skills that you can learn, practice, and refine during your college years—developed skills that you take with you from college into the world of work.

Skills are the key. In and of itself, a college degree won't help you solve a difficult financial or personnel problem in your firm. It won't enable you to sell computer equipment, put together an advertising campaign, understand new business opportunities in domestic or foreign markets, or negotiate a cooperative agreement with European or Japanese business partners. You cannot evoke the magic powers of a college degree to supervise an office of twenty or thirty people, to create a marketing plan, or to manage a new product launch involving millions of dollars.

What will help you are the skills, the insights, the capabilities, and the experiences that you acquire in college. These are the keys to success. These skills, together with the classroom knowledge ob-

Do You Have These Executive Skills?

Shortly after his son Tucker started his first job, Sommers White, president of his own management and financial consulting firm in Phoenix, wrote him a letter. Said the father to the son, "I thought you might like to see a list of some of the words I believe are used to describe managers who are the most sought after." His list follows. How many of these terms could you honestly use to describe yourself?

Cool • Wily • Canny • Gutsy • Tough • A star • Bright • Leader • Logical • Dynamic • Serious • Capable • Outgoing • Creative • Vigorous • Intuitive • Versatile • Efficient • Perceptive • Clean desk • Innovative • Personable • Determined • Aggressive • Keen minded • Intelligent • Charismatic • Wins loyalty • Gets results • Inspirational • Inexhaustible • Lots of flair • Gracious host • Goal oriented • Numbers person • Hides intensity • Good negotiator • Good storyteller • Boy Scout ethics • Leads by example • Unbelievable energy • Developer of talent • Unlimited potential • Sensitive to people • Fertile imagination • Good strategic thinker • Tremendous concentration • . . . . *and the most oft-used of all: High energy.*

Source: The Insider, Summer 1989, p. 5.

tained in a well-conceived degree program, will prepare you for the challenges of the 1990s and the twenty-first century.

Sommers White's list of executive or managerial qualities is interesting and most probably correct. Unfortunately, it doesn't necessarily help the aspiring student. More useful would be a list that categorizes these qualities into specific areas. Consequently we have chosen to organize many of these qualities and others into skill packages. We've tagged these skills as if they were people.

- The Great Communicator
- The Team Player
- The Technology Master
- The Problem Solver
- The Foreign Ambassador
- The Change Maker
- The Twenty-first-Century Leader

Let's take a quick introductory look at these people. We'll learn why companies in all industries are eager to hire them and why these skills are so important that they are the focus of the next seven chapters.

The Great Communicator

Business professionals spend most of their day in some form of communication. They communicate with each other about procedures and problems. They speak to customers, write memos, read manuals, attend meetings, and make presentations. In business, communication skills are more than important—*they are essential.* Numerous studies and reports on key "success skills" are unanimous. Business wants the Great Communicator—the individual who can read, write, speak, and listen. Let's look at some of the evidence.

- A 1988 survey of 113 officers of large U.S. corporations asked the respondents to identify the factors that "become more important to success as a college graduate employee progresses to middle or top positions in your company." The trait most often identified: verbal communication skills.

- A 1989 Stanford University study of the personal traits needed for future business success reached a similar conclusion. One of the respondents, John Callen, partner with executive recruiters Ward Howell International, stated, "The most sought-after skill, from the CEO down, is the ability to communicate with people."

- The American Management Association surveyed some 300 middle- and upper-level managers, asking what was the most often cited drawback of job applicants. The "inability to express oneself clearly" was the number-one response, cited by almost 60 percent of the respondents to this 1986 survey.

The answer is always the same, no matter which way the question is asked: Both large corporations and small businesses want people with effective communication skills.

Of course, the importance of communication skills should not be surprising. Tomorrow's corporate managers will be very different from their counterparts of today: They will spend less time giving orders and more time acting as facilitators and coaches. This has important consequences for all types of organizations. In manufacturing companies, for example, managers will have to draw together the skills, knowledge, and goodwill of engineers, designers, and hourly employees to create functional, top-quality products at reasonable, competitive prices. Such managers will play supporting roles by coordinating their subordinates' activities through communication efforts.

College has often been described in terms of the "ivory tower." But it is interesting that, in this case at least, the realities of the corporate world are accurately reflected in the views of college professors. The American Assembly of Collegiate Schools of Business (AACSB), the sole recognized accrediting agency for business schools, recently commissioned a major study of management education. The authors, former business school deans Lyman Porter and Lawrence McKibbin, surveyed business students, professors, deans, and corporate executives. One of their survey questions asked about the emphasis that is currently given and should be given to the development of various skills and personal characteristics in business programs. Table 2 summarizes the responses of business school faculty to this survey. Business school professors see communication skills as the area with the greatest discrepancy, the area where programs should do more to help students cultivate key competencies for the future. Both the corporate world and the college campus strongly believe that college graduates need to be better communicators.

We should also mention that the skill of getting your ideas across to other people, as well as discovering what people require, is not industry specific. Whether the person's field is accounting, advertising, engineering, or selling, individual effectiveness depends on a profi-

Table 2. Perspectives of Business School Faculty on the Emphasis Given to Skill Development in Their Own Programs

(percent checking "emphasized very much")

Skill	Current	Should Be	Difference
Written communication	12	81	69
Oral communication	8	71	63
Analytical	28	78	50
Decision making	20	68	48
Initiative	7	48	41
Leadership/interpersonal skills	11	52	41
Computer	18	52	34
Planning/organizing	12	42	30
Risk taking	3	27	24

Source: Lyman W. Porter and Lawrence E. McKibbin, *Management Education and Development: Drift or Thrust into the 21st Century* (New York: McGraw-Hill), 1988.

ciency in listening, reading, speaking, and writing skills. For example, many people assume that accountants need to know only "debits and credits." Yet a recent report, *Perspectives on Education: Capabilities for Success in the Accounting Profession,* developed jointly by the nation's largest (Big Six) accounting firms, said otherwise. In their concern for the "quality and number of accounting graduates available to the public accounting profession," the report's authors discussed communication skills in the following manner.

- Public accounting requires its practitioners to be able to transfer and receive information with ease.

- Practitioners must be able to present and defend their views through formal and informal, written and oral, presentation. They must be able to do so on a peer level with business executives.

- As the rate of change in the business world increases, so does the amount of information that must be gathered from outside sources. Practitioners must be able to listen effectively to gain information and understand opposing points of view. They also will need the ability to locate, obtain, and organize information from both human and electronic sources.

The evidence is indeed overwhelming. In the great talent search that industry conducts among graduating college seniors, one person will be more sought after than any of the others. That person is the Great Communicator.

The Team Player

Over the past two decades there has been a tremendous increase in the use of teams in industry. The Industrial Age tended to promote linear thinking—one thing after the other. Problems are solved in sequence, like materials moving down an assembly line to create a car or a coffee maker.

In the typical U.S. company the designers conceive and create the product, the engineers build it, the marketers promote it, and the sales force sells it. It is usually a linear process—again, one thing after the other. (See Fig. 3.) But what happens when the engineers say that an interesting feature included in the product by the designers will be exorbitantly expensive to build? It may drive up the final product cost, placing the price of the product out of the reach of the "target" market, say, a young family. The redesign and reengineering needed to eliminate that particular "problem" feature could take months.

But the Information Age is very different. It thrives on speed, flexibility, and nonlinear thinking. What if the designer, the engineer, and the product-marketing manager worked in the same room? What if they talked with each other daily, having frequent and informal conversations about their work? The "interesting feature" would be of immediate concern to the engineer and the marketer. The problem could be identified and resolved in a short period of time, perhaps in days rather than in weeks or months.

Let's look at a classic U.S. industry—automobiles—for an example of the costs of linear thinking. From the 1950s to the 1980s, U.S. automobile companies typically needed five years to develop a new car—to take it from initial conceptualization (specifications, pricing, competitive analysis) to production (engineering, design, manufacturing) and into distribution (marketing, promotion, and sales). In contrast to the old U.S. approach, Japanese car companies (Toyota in particular) have successfully reduced the total development time to three years. As Ross Perot, quoted at the start of this book, has said, "It takes five years to develop a new car in this country. Heck, we won World War II in four years."

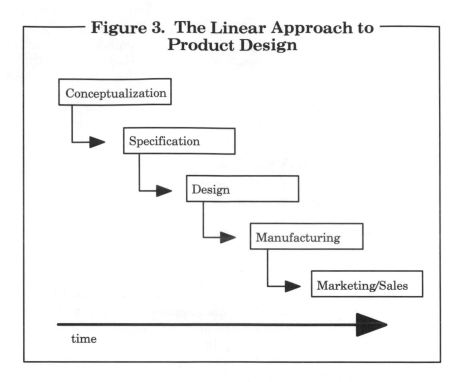

Figure 3. The Linear Approach to Product Design

Why the big difference? What accounts for the extra two years in Detroit? Observers suggest it is largely due to differences in organizational structure. Development teams work together in the Japanese companies, from conceptualization through marketing and sales. These groups talk with one another, providing essential information and important feedback that facilitate design and manufacturing and enhance marketing efforts and sales activities. (See Fig. 4.) This responsiveness is essential as styles, technology, and market opportunities change rapidly. Those two years can easily translate into a huge success or a dismal failure; they also translate into significant cost savings.

> *The winners of the nineties will be those firms who can develop a [corporate] culture that allows [organizations] to move faster, communicate more clearly, and involve everyone in a focused effort to serve ever more demanding customers. To move toward that winning [corporate] culture we have to create what we call a "boundaryless" company. We no longer have time to climb over barriers between functions like engineering and marketing or between people—hourly, salary, management and the like.*
>
> John F. Welch Jr., CEO, General Electric

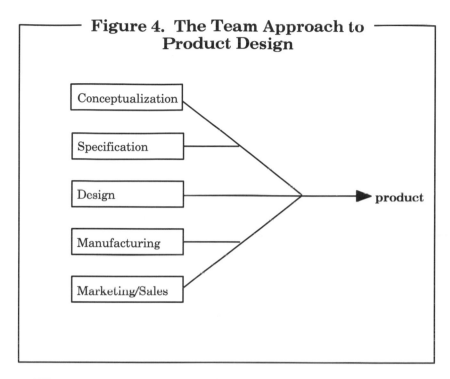

Figure 4. The Team Approach to Product Design

Whenever people work together, especially with different backgrounds, successful interaction depends upon effective interpersonal skills—getting along with others. Merely placing three people in the same room does not yield teamwork. Teamwork depends upon the ability of the individuals to pull together and focus on a common goal. The Team Player must recognize that people have unique personalities and that they come to common problems with different backgrounds and skills. The ability to evaluate the feelings, strengths, and flaws of others and respond appropriately is crucial.

More and more, teamwork skills are seen not so much as desirable but as required. The modern corporation can no longer afford to hire "five-year car" people; they need "three-year car" people. Consider the recent comment of Robert LoPresto, a senior partner with the personnel firm of Korn/Ferry International: "There are lots of brilliant people who can't relate with others. We replace that kind of person every day."

The Technology Master

The Information Age and technological advances fostered by the computer are intermeshed. The strong focus on the generation and use of information would not have occurred without an accompanying capability to store and convert data into useful information. Computer competence, therefore, involves the key computer-based skills individuals need to analyze and distribute information in the performance of their job.

According to one recent study, this key competence will become even more important in the future. A 1987 study by the College Placement Council, which collects and maintains information on trends and projections that affect career planning and placement, identified corporate perspectives on the "ideal job candidate of the 21st century." According to the council, newly hired managerial trainees must be computer competent, in addition to possessing well-developed communication and people skills. These new basic computer skills include:

- preparing comprehensive, literate, graphic-rich reports, memoranda, and other written documents;
- analyzing statistical and financial data and converting them into useful information;
- presenting information utilizing schematic drawings and business graphics that help convey key concepts and important issues;
- accessing electronic information libraries, corporate data banks, and other information resources (for example, Dow Jones On-Line Information Services, the Business Periodical Index, or a compact disk full of scientific or government data) and downloading information; and
- using electronic mail to communicate quickly and effectively with peers, supervisors, and clients—elsewhere in the building, across the company, or around the world.

Clearly this information orientation goes beyond the traditional financial, accounting, and management information system (MIS) operations of a company, large or small. For example, just as we have heard accounting students express disbelief that communication skills will be important to their future, we have also seen many business students attempt to avoid computers by majoring in marketing or management. Yet a 1987 study of marketing professionals suggests that managers cannot avoid computers. Indeed, there was virtually no area of marketing, from sales to distribution, in which managers did not spend considerable time using computers to process information. (See Table 3.)

As noted above, being computer literate does not necessarily mean that the business student (or marketing professional) needs expert

Table 3. Managerial Activities: The Importance and Use of Computers

(percentages)

Activity	Respondents Who Used Personal Computers	Respondents Who Used Mainframes	Avg. Pct. of Work Time on Activity
Forecasting Sales	38	20	11
Selling Activities	33	12	23
Promotional Strategy	32	7	19
Pricing Decisions	32	19	11
Product Development	30	5	16
Sales Force Management	25	20	21
Managing Inventory	22	36	11
Quality Control	21	8	10
Product Distribution	19	24	11

Source: John Mentzer, Camille Schuster, and David Roberts, "Microcomputer Versus Mainframe Usage by Marketing Professionals," *Journal of the Academy of Marketing Sciences,* Summer 1987, p. 1.

computer programming skills. As recently as five or ten years ago, programming skills were important not because managers did their own programming, but because they had to communicate with programmers about their specific project needs and the design of software. In other words, for nontechnical staff, familiarity with programming involved acquiring a communication skill for working with the computing professionals who ran the corporate computers and information systems.

The microcomputer revolution of the 1980s changed this in very dramatic ways. The trend toward computer applications (such as word processing, graphics, and spreadsheets) now means that people can be sophisticated users without being computer programmers. And business has come to view these skills—competence with key applications like word processing, graphics, and spreadsheets—as essential. Business professionals must possess a set of computer skills that allow them to use application software to enhance their own job performance through information. And if we haven't convinced you so far of the inevitability of the computer-driven Information Age, let's end this section with an observation by Ralph Gormory, former head of research at IBM, who predicts with "total confidence"

Drawing by Ziegler; © 1990 *The New Yorker* Magazine, Inc.

that computers will become 100 times cheaper in the next two decades. This means that most of the Information Revolution is still
ahead of us.

The Problem Solver

For information to be useful, it must be converted into knowledge;
that is, individuals must analyze and integrate the data, then act on
the implications. The Problem Solver, therefore, becomes the perfect
complement to the Technology Master. Our marketing professional,
for example, can use his or her technology skills to identify a marketing opportunity for a new product or to resolve a problem confronting
a current product. Say there is a dramatic decline in sales in one of the
districts. Since it is crucial in business to monitor the success or
failure of sales activities, a savvy marketing manager will have an
"early detection" information system in place.

But the computer is not capable of responding to the next logical
question once we have detected a sales decline. And that is "Why?"
Problem solving or analytical thinking, therefore, can be defined as
the mental activity leading from an unsatisfactory state to a more
desired satisfactory state. The process extends from a clear statement
of the problem to generating a solution and implementing it. Our

marketing manager is acting as the Problem Solver when he or she uses the information available to identify the sales decline problem and then implements a solution to get sales back on track.

In the section on the Great Communicator we noted the results of a survey of 113 corporate officers on the factors that "become more important to success as a college graduate employee progresses to middle or top positions in your company." Having communication skills was the trait most frequently cited by the survey participants. The other traits that were deemed important, in rank order, were:

- Ability to identify and formulate problems
- Willingness to assume responsibility
- Interpersonal skills
- Reasoning ability
- Creativity
- Ability to function independently

Two of these traits, "ability to identify and formulate problems" and "reasoning ability," are important aspects of problem solving. The Problem Solver, therefore, is not merely someone who can generate a solution to a problem but someone who also has a specific set of capabilities for making sound choices in an increasingly complex world. In the same way that corporations look for individuals with good communication and interpersonal skills, they also look for ones with strong analytical skills. And along with judging communication and interpersonal skills in interviews, corporations have become adept at testing potential employees' problem-solving abilities as well.

A few examples will help. Denise Scheid, manager of human resources at the Chubb Group of Insurance Companies in Irvine, California, comes at the issue of decision-making skills directly: "Underwriters make million-dollar decisions every day. We can't afford to hire people who don't know how to analyze situations and make informed decisions." So one of the first screening devices used at Chubb is a little test. Interviewees are asked to respond to the following scenarios.

What concerns and/or questions would you have if you were evaluating (for an insurance policy) a business that:

1. Manufactures ladders.
2. Manufactures sheet metal used primarily for storage tanks.

Your initial reaction might be "What do I know about insurance? How can I possibly answer?" Well, Chubb does not interview only finance or insurance majors. In fact, its interviewers are not that interested in whether you know anything about the industry. What they are looking for is your thought process. For example, you might want to know what the ladders are made of or how long the company has been in business. Perhaps your concern for potential liability might also lead you to ask whether there are warning labels on the ladders. How about the sheet-metal manufacturer? Are the tanks usually above or below ground? What's in those tanks, anyway?

Chase Manhattan Bank, also interested in the thought process of its future employees, employs the "analytical interview."

Chase Manhattan Bank

According to Stanley Burns, vice president of Chase Manhattan Bank, Chase's recruiting efforts generally include several types of interviews. An initial interview, either on campus or in New York, determines whether in a general way overall abilities, motivation, and interpersonal skills seem to fit their requirements. Candidates are subsequently interviewed by a human resources specialist who (1) informs the candidate about Chase's organizational structure and career opportunities and (2) determines if the candidate meets the general criteria for a specific business unit. Finally, the candidate is interviewed by managers who assess very specific analytical skills.

In describing the history of the "analytical interview," Burns notes that "In the mid-1970s we started to look more closely at the specific mental abilities that are required for successful performance, both in our training program and in management jobs thereafter. We recognized that while many job requirements will vary from business unit to business unit, there are certain mental abilities in common that are needed if strong analytical skills are to develop."

Consequently Chase Manhattan studied the content and structure of its training program and its entry-level management jobs to identify critical mental abilities. Six abilities were determined to be necessary: memory, learning speed, logical reasoning, divergent thinking, convergent thinking, and affinity for numbers. The bank then developed a series of cases that could be used in an interview to focus on the mental abilities. The cases, with an interviewer's probing questions, are used to see if the candidate has the basic problem-solving capabilities necessary for success at Chase Manhattan.

Source: Stanley Burns, "From Student to Banker: Observations from the Chase Bank," from *Association of American Colleges and the National Endowment for the Humanities Conference,* Princeton, New Jersey, April 1983.

The process is straightforward for insurance companies, advertising agencies, accounting firms, and banks. Find people who have a set of basic skills, such as problem-solving capabilities, and then provide training and job experiences that build on that base.

The Foreign Ambassador

A global economy is not a thing of the future. It is now. And how has this nation approached this new world of interdependence? From 1940 to 1970, the United States enjoyed a period of extraordinary internal growth. A rapidly growing population and the economic boom following World War II encouraged us to focus on domestic production and consumption of products. The size of the U.S. markets, our geographic isolation from the European and Asian continents, and our seemingly inexhaustible natural resources were sufficient to keep our focus inward. Consequently over the past twenty years, as Japan and other countries have begun to stretch their international economic muscles, the United States has been slow to adjust. And the results are obvious.

What can be done? The changing role of the United States in the world demands that we develop a better understanding of the international scene in which we live and work. In a 1987 article, "The Trade Crisis Begins at Home," Thomas Keller, dean of the School of Business at Duke University, discusses the issue of trade barrier legislation. He notes that U.S. business has continually failed to do overseas what it has historically done best here: understand its customers' needs. His solution to the "What can be done?" question is simple: "For one thing, we must train managers to be less insular." Keller goes on to say:

> From my perspective as an academic dean, I think the problem relates to education. American business schools, which should be training a new generation of internationally adept managers, are not doing enough to help students understand the complexities of foreign marketplaces. As a result, we are sowing the seeds for a continued bitter harvest.

These are not isolated words of doom. An impending global economy suggests that Americans need to adjust their perceptions of reality to incorporate a broader understanding of the world around us. (You may want to judge your understanding by taking the I.Q. test on page 36.) We need to shift our view outward. One business author recently wrote: "America's ability to compete in an increasingly interdependent world requires well-trained professionals skilled in dealing with other cultures, languages, business and economic systems." And a college administrator comments in a leading academic journal: "The

```
┌──────────── Test Your International I.Q. ────────────┐
```

Test Your International I.Q.

1. Which modern-day country shares the same approximate boundaries as ancient Persia?
   A. Oman   B. Saudi Arabia   C. Iran
2. Which of the following countries has the most capital invested in the United States?
   A. Britain   B. West Germany   C. Japan
3. How much does a Moscow subway ride cost in U.S. dollars?
   A. $.07   B. $.75   C. $2.50
4. What famous economist made his fortune by investing in international exchange rates?
   A. John Maynard Keynes   B. Adam Smith
   C. John Kenneth Galbraith
5. Which two countries have received great trade and tax benefits from their Maquiladora activities?
   A. United States and Nicaragua   B. United States and Mexico
   C. Canada and Panama
6. Which Soviet republic is most likely to be designated a special economic zone for USSR trade in the very near future?
   A. Estonia   B. Georgia   C. Siberia
7. What is the smallest country in the world?
   A. Vatican City   B. Liechtenstein   C. New Caledonia
8. In 1982 the British and the Argentines met in war over a group of islands in the South Atlantic. By what two names are those islands known?
   A. The Falklands and the Magellans
   B. The Falklands and the Malvinas
   C. The Falklands and the Azores
9. What place is the site of the next Summer Olympics?
   A. Sao Paulo, Brazil   B. Nairobi, Kenya   C. Barcelona, Spain
10. In Israel today, the Likud and the Labor parties are:
    A. Different names for the same political party.
    B. Political parties that no longer have power.
    C. The two most prominent political parties.

Bonus:
Name the person who has helped China sign more than $1 billion in joint ventures and trade agreements.
   A. Virginia Kamsky   B. Armand Hammer   C. Donald Trump

Answers: (score 2 points for each correct answer)
   1. C   3. A   5. B   7. A   9. C
   2. A   4. A   6. A   8. B   10. C   Bonus: A

If you scored:
18–22: The Foreign Service would be glad to have you.
14–18: You're a world-class tourist.
8–14:   You can pretend to be a world-class tourist.
0–8:   You could be a baggage handler for TWA.

Source: Reprinted by permission of the International Association of Students in Economics and Business Management (called AISEC), New York. An exhibit authored by Sandre Cunha and Richard Pannenmann, appearing in *Business Today,* Winter 1989, p. 4.

evidence is clear that colleges and universities have a major responsibility to help our students and our society to better prepare to live and work in a world of increasingly interdependent culture and people."

Again and again, U.S. companies have lost business opportunities overseas, even when U.S. products have been very good and priced right. Why? Because Americans repeatedly—and incorrectly—think that successful products and marketing strategies in domestic markets will also be effective and successful in other countries. The mistakes can only continue if business professionals are not properly trained in language and cultural skills. The world *is* shrinking; economic systems are increasingly interdependent. The Foreign Ambassador will be an increasingly valued person in U.S. corporations that recognize global competition and look to expanding global markets.

The Change Maker

Innovation is a search for change. Perhaps it's a different way of doing things or merely a way to do things faster or cheaper. Innovation and change are the specific tools of modern business. Regardless of the industry, businesses require a continuous, unceasing flow of creative ideas in order to compete and prosper. Innovation is needed to increase productivity and efficiency, to improve the quality of goods and services, to develop new products and processes, and to launch effective marketing strategies. A business organization that is not interested in innovation will not stay viable in the modern business world for very long. Competition is too fierce, technology is changing too rapidly, and consumer preferences shift too quickly to allow any company the luxury of becoming "fat and happy." In a period of rapid change, a world turned upside down, companies have little choice: *They must innovate or die.*

The reason for this "urgency" is that creativity, innovation, and entrepreneurism are not common characteristics in today's workplace. Many, if not most, people who are established in a business are resistant to new ways. They are often apathetic and hostile to change. Their knee-jerk response to anything new or different is "We've already tried that" or "It'll never work." In spite of the pressing need for people who can effect change, U.S. industry has too many people who feel insecure in the face of change. We get comfortable with things as they are.

One classic example will do quite nicely. There is a famous industrial company, nameless here, which had to make a very, very delicate adjustment in the final stage of manufacturing a product. A huge valve on the wall had to be turned at a specific point in this very

Roadblocks to Innovation

To understand better why creativity fares so poorly in business, we have to consider the various roadblocks that exist. The pathways of most new ideas are blocked by:

- resistance to change;
- premature and uninformed judgments;
- neophobia—the dread of anything new or novel, fear of the unknown;
- sense of embarrassment or humiliation that accompanies the admission that existing products or procedures are inferior to new proposals;
- caution—it's safer to have the "me-too-later" attitude;
- threat to the predictability and continuity on which all businesses are based—a new idea frequently represents a potential or real disruption of this continuity; the unwritten principle in business requires that disruptions be strictly controlled or held to a minimum, no matter what they are;
- anticipation of the extra trouble in handling and implementing new ideas: "We have enough work as it is."; and
- politics—new ideas frequently pose a threat to the organizational stature and vested interests of managers who are anxious to maintain the existing hierarchical structure.

Source: Eugene Raudsepp, *Growth Games for the Creative Manager* (New York: Putnam Publishing, 1987), p. 10.

delicate process, and it could be turned by only two or three people in the plant. Anyone else who dared touch the valve was shooed away or risked being fired. This "craft" was passed down from generation to generation. After many years the plant was rebuilt, and it was discovered that the valve, the one that required the delicate adjustment, wasn't connected to anything!

In the face of such opposition, what is it that successful, innovative companies, large or small, have in common? *The most distinguishing characteristic of such companies is that they are filled with creative people.* Businesses, especially smaller ones, grow because they are on a high-protein diet, one that constantly feeds them with new ideas. Instead of blindly following established procedures or relying on time-tested techniques, successful companies have a strong core of people who are looking beyond current solutions. They are alert to new techniques and methods and are willing to take risks. These people are not only willing to accept change, they seek it out. Or as one industry consultant suggests, "They have a divine discontent with the status quo."

Johnson & Johnson, for example, best known to most people as a health-care supply company, has introduced more than 200 new products in the United States over the past five years. At Minnesota Mining and Manufacturing (3M Company) new products bubble up at an astonishing rate. 3M researchers are encouraged to spend 15 percent of their time pursuing pet projects that might have a payoff down the line. In 1987 more than one fourth of 3M's worldwide sales came from new products—products that did not exist in 1982!

The need for innovators in U.S. industry has also evolved in another way. It used to be that "change" was the domain of a handful of upper-level managers. They were the entrepreneurs with innovation skills. But it has become evident that change, and the need for it as part of the culture of a company, is too important to be left to the bosses. In fact, Tom Peters in his national bestseller, *Thriving on Chaos: Handbook for a Management Revolution,* goes so far as to state: "No skill is more important than the corporate capacity to change per se. The company's most urgent task, then, is to learn to welcome—beg for, demand—innovation from everyone."

The Twenty-first-Century Leader

One authority has collected 350 different definitions of leadership, including one from President Harry Truman: "[Leadership is] the ability to get other people to do what they don't want to do, and like it." Although the definition of leadership is fuzzy, its impact on an organization is not. There simply are no successful companies that are not jam-packed with leaders. Leaders excite and inspire others. They are dreamers with a vision and a strong work ethic. They turn a job into a challenge. They make it fun.

U.S. businesses desperately need leaders. One recent *Industry Week* article was titled "U.S. Managers No Longer No. 1: Better Leadership Is the Reason for Japanese Dominance." A *Fortune* magazine title was no more subtle: "Wanted: Leaders Who Can Make a Difference." At the same time, a torrent of books has hit the bookstore shelves —*Why Leaders Can't Lead, The Leadership Factor, The Leadership Challenge, The Transformational Leader,* among others. These books and articles arrive at the same basic conclusion: Leadership is a pivotal force behind successful organizations.

As described in Chapter 1, major changes are under way in American corporations. U.S. companies will run "leaner and meaner" in the 1990s; they will employ fewer midlevel managers. They must be more innovative and flexible. They will need to respond to the increasing competition of global markets. However, the problem with many of the businesses that fail to respond to this new vision is that they are overmanaged and underled. USC professor Warren Bennis, a nationally recognized authority on leadership, explains the difference between managers and leaders.

> *"To manage" means "to bring about, to accomplish, to have charge or responsibility for, to conduct." "Leading" is "influencing, guiding in direction, course, action, opinion." The distinction is crucial. Managers are people who do things right and leaders are people who do the right thing.*

What becomes apparent is that as management is replaced by leadership, authority is delegated to more and more people within the company. They become empowered. The burden of responsibility is shifted onto their shoulders. Quality is not the responsibility of a quality control inspector; new product ideas are not the responsibility of the president, CEO, or some committee. Leadership at the top must be contagious in that in order to be successful, there must be leadership at the bottom as well. Lee Iacocca's leadership job is to create a vision for all of Chrysler's employees. He doesn't have time to control or manage his people. To be successful, Chrysler has had to rely on the leaders up and down the production line to take responsibility for quality and new ways of doing things. Such leadership, embedded in the hearts and minds of everyone, provides the enthusiasm, the spirit of success. Or as Bennis has pointed out, "There isn't a company in America that wouldn't benefit from a little less efficiency and a lot more inspiration."

The successful business graduate of the 1990s cannot be a follower, one who is content to follow instructions, not make any mistakes, and collect a paycheck on Friday. This is reinforced by the following Seven Keys to Business Leadership.

❖

The Seven Keys to Business Leadership

In one of the many new "leadership" articles, Larry Meares, an internal consultant with Leaseway Transportation Corporation in Cleveland, begins, "What makes a good business leader?" He then proceeds to detail fifty recommendations that represent his personal list of leadership qualities. They include pointers like "Insist on intellectual honesty from everyone" and "Hold everyone to his or her commitments." A leaner list follows.

1. *Trust your subordinates.* You can't expect them to go all out for you if they think you don't believe in them.
2. *Develop a vision.* Some executives' suspicions to the contrary, planning for the long term pays off. And people want to follow someone who knows where he or she is going.
3. *Keep your cool.* The best leaders show their mettle under fire.
4. *Encourage risk.* Nothing demoralizes the troops like knowing that the slightest failure could jeopardize their entire career.
5. *Be an expert.* From the boardroom to mail room, everyone had better understand that you know what you're talking about.
6. *Invite dissent.* Your people aren't giving you their best or learning how to lead if they are afraid to speak up.
7. *Simplify.* You need to see the big picture in order to set a course, communicate it, and maintain it. Keep the details at bay.

Source: Kenneth Labich, "The Seven Keys to Business Leadership," *Fortune*, October 24, 1988, p. 58.

The Guarantee

Our first chapter described a crazy new world. What was successful yesterday offers no guarantee of success either today or tomorrow. Things are changing too rapidly—a world turned upside down. In this chapter we have looked at those special skills and talents needed not only to survive but to thrive in the years to come.

You may be saying to yourself that you have already decided to pursue a career in accounting or major in management information systems, so you're set. Wrong! The decision to major in business doesn't let you off the hook. It doesn't isolate—or protect—you from the demands of a rapidly changing new world. Industry wants more than another employee with a college degree. It wants the Great Communicator. It wants the Problem Solver. It wants the Foreign Ambassador. And it will get them. Because with more than a million college graduates looking for jobs each year (one fourth of them with business degrees), both large corporations and small businesses can afford to look beyond the first line of a resume, the one that shows your degree and alma mater.

The next seven chapters are *action items*. They translate the general skills that we have described into a series of steps that you can take—*while in college*—to guarantee your future in business. Each chapter also profiles a specific college or university in order to show you how these action items can be applied to your school. Without further delay, let's proceed.

II

The Challenge

3

The Great Communicator

Communication Skills Inventory

Speak effectively to another individual • Write factual material clearly and concisely • Read with comprehension/speed • Question effectively • Write persuasively • Speak effectively to groups • Listen intently/objectively • Explain concepts well • Critique, edit, and proofread • Express feelings appropriately

If you are in college or applying to a college, it is safe to assume that you can read, write, and speak. You can probably even do a decent job of listening. So what's the big deal? You've been communicating all your life; people seem to understand you. The problem is largely one of expectations. Your friends, the gas station attendant, the person behind the counter at the donut shop—they are not all that concerned about your spoken grammar. You probably don't write to any of these people, so writing skills may not seem to be much of a problem, either.

But such is not the case at General Motors, IBM, General Electric, an advertising agency, or an accounting firm. Sales representatives who aren't skilled at listening simply do not last long. Junior analysts who write "butchered memos" can forget about promotions. The botched presentation is not soon forgotten.

Consider the viewpoint of Roger Smith, former chairman of General Motors: "Organizational leaders are first and foremost in the human relations and communications business. No other item on the chief executive's duty list has more leverage on the organization's prospects."

SNAPSHOTS

"Damn it. I wouldn't accept this level of writing from someone who was working for me. This is critical. We need people who can write a decent one-page memo." Tony Branch, vice president of academic affairs at Golden Gate University, has heard these words all too often. They are the frustrated descriptions his adjunct faculty—many of whom are top industry executives in San Francisco—use to describe the writing skills of their students. For years Branch has listened to the concerns of senior executives; the conversations have been monotonously the same. Says Branch: "We sit around having lunch and discuss their students. Almost without exception, even from people in information systems or banking, it doesn't matter, they say that the students can't express themselves, especially in writing."

One of Branch's occasional lunch companions is Bernard Hargadon, president of McKesson International, a large food-products firm with offices across the United States and the world. One day each week Hargadon leaves his McKesson office after work to walk the several blocks to Golden Gate University, where he teaches a class in international management. From the corporate boardroom to the college classroom, the message is the same. Hargadon says, "Reams have been written about the functional skills—marketing, production, accounting, and so on—but underlying all of these is that single, most important 'other' skill, the ability to communicate. Why? Well, in the final analysis, what other verifiable evidence of an individual's intellect is there?" Branch agrees: "I personally think that if you can't write well, particularly when you have difficulties constructing paragraphs that flow together and reach a clear, concise conclusion, this suggests that the overall conceptual thinking is muddled and not worth much. There is a real relationship. It's not just a skill which would be nice to have. Good writing is reflective of sound thinking and problem-solving activities."

And don't think that this is just the basis for noontime lunch discussions. It is clearly more than that. According to Hargadon, "When hiring, and irrespective of the position to be filled, my principal focus is, and always has been, on how well the individual communicates, particularly in writing. Academic degrees, functional skills, and the like are of interest to me as well, but secondarily."

Liberal arts colleges have long made the case that English courses—writing, composition, and literature—and classes in public speaking were tremendous preparation for a career. Business schools know the importance of strong communication skills. College officials conduct surveys among Fortune 500 companies to determine their communication needs. Professors regularly interact with their counterparts in industry. Everyone—and we mean everyone—is in agreement. *Communication skills can make or break a career—and a firm.* In fact, a 1988 U.S. Department of Labor report on "the skills employers want" notes that while reading and writing are essential communication tools, *listening* and *speaking* are the most common form of interaction and communication. The average person spends 9 percent of communication time engaged in writing, 13 percent in reading, 23 percent in speaking, and over half—55 percent—in listening. (See Fig. 5.)

Jan Carlzon, president of Scandinavian Airlines (SAS), knows that a good leader spends more time speaking—informing, persuading, and inspiring—than doing anything else. From his first day at SAS he made communicating, particularly with his employees, a top priority. In fact, as Carlzon has noted, "During the first year I spent exactly half of my working hours 'out in the field' talking to SAS people. The word going around was that anytime three employees gathered, Jan Carlzon would probably show up and begin talking with them. It was my way of accepting responsibility and showing that my enthusiasm and involvement were genuine."

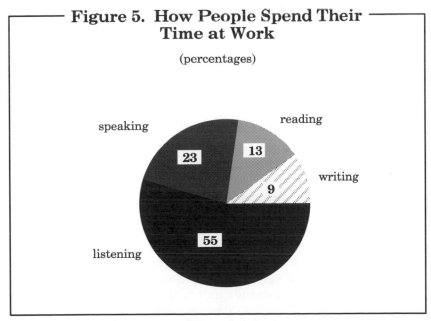

Figure 5. How People Spend Their Time at Work

(percentages)

speaking · 23
reading · 13
writing · 9
listening · 55

Source: Workplace Basics, U.S. Department of Labor, 1988, p. 11.

While speaking is essential, listening may become the key managerial talent of the 1990s. The cover story of the March 12, 1990, issue of *Business Week* screams "KING CUSTOMER . . . At Companies That Listen Hard and Respond Fast, Bottom Lines Thrive." The story describes how companies have begun to realize that in a supercompetitive global economy, so-so merchandise and take-it-or-leave-it service form a straight road to bankruptcy. How do you create products and services that customers can't get enough of? You listen. To learn more about service, for example, executives are putting in stints at the "front line." At Xerox Corporation, executives spend one day a month taking complaints from customers about machines, bills, and services. At Hyatt Corporation hotels, senior executives put in time as bellhops. Many companies are using small groups of customers, called focus groups, to help them design new, need-satisfying products.

Tom Peters, an internationally known management guru and coauthor of the award-winning book *In Search of Excellence,* devotes an entire chapter in his 1987 book, *Thriving on Chaos,* to becoming "obsessed with listening." First and foremost, Peters notes that "listening, like so many simple ideas, turns out to be anything but simple . . . it must be practiced." Although Peters' prescriptions for listening skills are oriented primarily toward corporations concerned about "staying close to the customer" (that is, trying to understand the needs of their customers by listening carefully), his observations apply to interpersonal behavior as much as to corporate behavior:

> *Become transparent to [that is, listen to] customers [peers, supervisors, subordinates]. . . . Listen frequently. Listen systematically—and unsystematically. Listen for facts and for perceptions. Listen naively. Use as many listening techniques as you can possibly conjure up. . . .*

A Collegiate Overview

There are two ways that business schools or departments have chosen to address the communication skills issue. One might be called the *integration approach.* The second is the *focused communications model.*

The Integration Approach

Many colleges attempt to incorporate basic communication skills into their standard courses. For example, a management course may have a research assignment that requires a class presentation, or a marketing course may require students to conduct a series of consumer interviews ("listening" skills). One accounting educator, Professor Pernell Hewing of the University of Wisconsin–Whitewater, offers the following guidelines to other professors for integrating these skills into accounting courses.

1. Assess writing and speaking skills.
   a. Have student write one-page essay on reason for choosing accounting as a career.
   b. Have student write an autobiography.
   c. Have student write a paragraph on a given topic.
   d. Have each student introduce and talk for a minute or more about self.
2. Practical suggestions for providing writing and speaking experiences for accounting students.
   a. Give essay examinations and evaluate them for basic language skills.
   b. Have students interview practicing accountants and write a brief report.
   c. Team with communications professor to improve written and oral skills using an accounting context. Make assignments on particular accounting topics that involve writing, and have communications teacher evaluate the written output.
   d. Encourage class oral participation.
   e. Make oral report assignment tied to club activity, e.g., Beta Alpha Psi, Alobeam Society, or other group.

From our experience there are several problems with this model. First, not enough college professors use it. It is the uncommon teacher who goes beyond simply lecturing students about the technical aspects of a specific field. In an accounting class you learn accounting techniques, in finance you discuss the tools of finance. Specialization in most academic departments has led to the segmentation of responsibility: Writing instructors, not accountants, are responsible for evaluating student writing. Comparatively few faculty members from other fields are expected to invest the time to provide critical feedback on students' communication skills.

But the second problem is even more serious. Students often avoid these classes—ones that require term papers or class presentations—like the plague. Instead, they flock to courses that offer multiple-choice midterm exams and finals. These courses, and the tests used in these classes, are easy and quick and provide many students the anonymity that they seem to seek so desperately. But the plain fact is that no one is going to base your quarterly performance or annual merit raise at XYZ Corporation on a multiple-choice examination at the end of the fiscal year. You are graded each and every day on a thousand small interactions that involve communication: a memo sent to a supervisor, a phone conversation with a customer, and so forth. People judge you on their *perceptions* of your skills and performance. These perceptions are formed in elevator conversations, comments at meetings, and so on. So courses that force you to communicate are critical to your future success. Don't hide from them; don't run the other way. Seek them out, and read, write, speak, and listen.

The Focused Communications Model

An alternative to this integrative approach has been the development of specific communications courses, often in the business school or separate communications department. A 1987 study conducted by faculty members at Central Michigan University indicates that more than three quarters of all colleges that have undergraduate business programs offered a course in business communications. The survey also noted that most class time was devoted to the following (ranked) activities: (1) correspondence (letters, memos), (2) report writing, (3) general communication theory, (4) employment process (resume writing and interviewing), and (5) oral presentations.

Criticism about the standard business communications course typically focuses on two issues. The first is the perceived overemphasis on writing skills; for instance, we have noted that over half of a person's time at work is devoted to listening. Ineffective listening costs American business billions each year. Because of poor listening, customers' and employees' needs are ignored, letters have to be retyped, appointments have to be rescheduled, orders have to be reshipped, and *ideas are distorted by as much as 80 percent as they travel through communications channels.* (For a humorous example of distortion, see page 51.)

Evidence of poor listening skills is not as readily noticeable as poor writing or speaking skills. In fact, poor listeners appear to equate "talking" with power. They do not realize that the person who is able to listen carefully, understand thoroughly, evaluate logically, and react intelligently is the one who possesses the real power. But while listening is the communication skill *most used,* it is also the skill that is the *least taught.*

The second criticism is that much of the emphasis on writing is directed internally—toward memos and reports that stay *within* an organization. But as we have pointed out repeatedly, the successful business professional of the 1990s must be responsive to customer needs: a two-way flow of information. For example, a study published in the *Journal of Education for Business* (1987) by Arizona State University professor Stephen Golen, focused on communication

Distortion

Distortion is a problem in all organizations, as can be seen as information is imparted from one party to another in this story.

A COLONEL issued the following directive to his EXECUTIVE OFFICER: "Tomorrow evening at approximately 2000 hours Halley's Comet will be visible in this area, an event that occurs only once every seventy-five years. Have the men fall out in the battalion area in fatigues, and I will explain this rare phenomenon to them. In case of rain, we will not be able to see anything, so assemble the men in the theater, and I will show them films of it."

EXECUTIVE OFFICER TO COMPANY COMMANDER: "By order of the colonel, tomorrow at 2000 hours, Halley's Comet will appear above the battalion area. If it rains, fall the men out in fatigues. Then march to the theater, where the rare phenomenon will take place, something that occurs only once every seventy-five years."

COMPANY COMMANDER TO LIEUTENANT: "By order of the colonel in fatigues at 2000 hours tomorrow evening, the phenomenal Halley's Comet will appear in the theater. In case of rain in the battalion area, the colonel will give another order, something that occurs once every seventy-five years."

LIEUTENANT TO SERGEANT: "Tomorrow at 2000 hours, the colonel will appear in the theater with Halley's Comet, something that happens every seventy-five years. If it rains, the colonel will order the comet into the battalion area in fatigues."

SERGEANT TO SQUAD: "When it rains tomorrow at 2000 hours, the phenomenal 75-year-old General Halley, accompanied by the colonel, will drive his Comet through the battalion area theater in fatigues."

Source: John W. Gould, "Quotations That Liven a Business Communication Course," *The Bulletin,* December 1985, p. 32.

barriers in banking: "With many college graduates entering the banking profession annually, communications instructors, as well as training instructors in banking, need to be aware of those barriers that managerial bank personnel may experience when dealing with customers." Interestingly, the results of the study relate to the previous problem of listening skills, since a dimension of "closed-mindedness and distractions" was viewed to be the most serious by

Effective Listening Skills

Effective listening, according to a 1985 Committee of the American Business Communication Association, can be taught. Instructional activities in listening can be classified into areas: (1) those devised to help students diagnose their listening abilities, (2) those designed to help students understand active listening, and (3) those developed to help build better listening skills. Effective listening requires that listeners:

- consciously exert effort in listening;
- resist distractions;
- seek areas of interest in what the speaker is saying;
- exercise their minds by not avoiding difficult material;
- judge content, not delivery or mannerisms;
- listen for central themes, not isolated facts;
- maintain open minds;
- defer evaluation of the speaker's remarks until comprehension is complete;
- be flexible and selective in notetaking; and
- capitalize on their thought speed.

---

bank managers. This communication barrier included such items as "tendency not to listen," "having too many intermediate receivers between sender and intended receiver of information," and "lack of feedback."

More recently, a second course in organizational communications has also been developed at some institutions. This course focuses on the personal, group, and organizational factors that influence communication in a business setting. Again, such courses usually require a significant amount of writing, speaking, and listening—through research reports, presentations, and interviews.

Outside the business school, students can begin to focus on either writing or oral communication. Writing skills, of course, can be sharpened most easily in the English department and, with those schools that have one, in a journalism department. Oral skills can be acquired through course work offered in a communications department or theater. Let's look more closely at these departments and their relevant course offerings.

English

Twenty years ago there was but one English department on most campuses. This one English department taught everything from composition to contemporary fiction, from rhetoric to Shakespeare. But on many campuses today the English department is a house divided. On one side of the divide are the traditional literature courses; the writing program sits on the other side. Virtually every college or university now has either a freshman writing program or a series of basic composition courses that are required for all students. These courses teach the analysis of writing styles and structure. Skillful argumentation and revision techniques are also a part of these courses.

Beyond these introductory courses, many colleges offer a more advanced composition course that is of particular importance to business students: *rhetoric*. The discipline of rhetoric—the art of using language effectively—goes back to Aristotle's famous essay on the subject 2,500 years ago. While some aspects of rhetoric are usually discussed in introductory courses, the subject matter of rhetoric deals with the full range of discourse. This involves exposition (we want to explain or inform about something), argument (we want to convince somebody), description (we want to tell what a thing looked like, sounded like, or felt like), and narration (we want to tell what happened). The one-page memo circulated by a sales manager or a product manager is an exercise in rhetoric. The sales manager needs *to inform* sales representatives about a new policy or sales program; the product manager needs *to convince* upper-level management that more advertising support is required.

Other writing courses in English can be divided essentially into two categories: those that are data driven and those that are not. By "data driven" we mean writing that is done to explain a set of information, perhaps the results of a consumer survey or an accounting audit. Courses in expository writing and in business and technical writing are data driven and more important to the business student than creative writing courses that stress shorter fiction assignments.

Journalism

A journalism department is generally found only in larger universities. And often it does not exist alone. Many colleges have departments of communications and journalism. At others the department of journalism also includes advertising classes, which at other institutions are offered in the business school. If, as F. Scott Fitzgerald once wrote, "All good writing is swimming under water and holding your breath," it requires a good deal of practice—or just plain hard work.

An excellent way to practice is by taking courses in newspaper reporting and writing or in feature writing. Such courses require students to engage in the hard work of observing, describing, and being concise. People in business are busy. Their time is valuable. No one, whether it's your boss or your client, has the time to try to figure out what you are attempting to say.

If the journalism department offers advertising courses, another way to practice writing is by enrolling in a course in advertising copy writing. Once more, such courses teach students to write in a clear, concise, and persuasive manner.

Communications

As in the case of journalism, a separate department of communications is usually found only at larger institutions. And even then the department can have many varied components: mass communications (including radio, television, and the print media) and speech communications; sometimes it is even combined with the theater department (as it is at our profiled college, Nebraska Wesleyan University). Beyond the introductory course, there are a host of communications courses that a business student needs to consider seriously.

For example, a basic course in public speaking is designed to improve the ability to speak before groups in order to inform and persuade. Do business people engage in speaking before groups? Bankers, stockbrokers, manufacturers, and management consultants are always making presentations. Sales representatives "pitch" products and services to buyers and purchasing agents. CEOs give speeches at stockholder meetings and make statements to the press. Frankly, it is hard to imagine a more important course in college for the future business professional than a class in public speaking.

Other classes that are also useful include those in persuasion or in argumentation and debate. These upper-level courses include the more advanced study of reasoning, strategy, and oral advocacy. Again, the most important aspect of these courses, like advanced writing courses, is that they involve active learning. There is minimal lecturing by a professor. Instead, students debate issues and make speeches—they practice the craft.

Theater

One of Shakespeare's most famous quotations (from *As You Like It*) states, "All the world's a stage and all the men and women merely players." When a junior executive makes a presentation before a group of vice presidents, the boardroom becomes his or her stage. The lights come up, the audience hushes, and the pressure is on to perform. Our junior executive is playing a role, that of the supersharp expert. There is no doubt that this is very "live" theater.

At most institutions students can take one or two acting courses to prepare themselves for the rigors of the stage—*and business.* The first course usually entails the basic techniques of acting, including actor preparation and role creation. A second course often expands into improvisation and movement or the techniques of connecting nonverbal communications to a script.

Campus Profile
Nebraska Wesleyan University

Nebraska Wesleyan University is a small, private liberal arts college. It has all those things that are typically associated with such a school—about 1,200 students (90 percent of whom come from Nebraska), a 15:1 student-faculty ratio, and a suburban location with guaranteed on-campus housing. As a liberal arts institution, it has quite broad general education requirements. It requires course work in seven areas: communications and symbolic thought (English and computing), humanistic studies (literature, philosophy, and religion), fine arts (art, music, and theater), biological and physical science (biology and chemistry), social aspects of American culture (history and sociology), cultural perspectives (a language or regional studies), and a seminar called Attitudes and Values.

A candidate for a business degree at Nebraska Wesleyan will take a minimum of twelve business courses. The interesting thing about these courses, which is true at most liberal arts institutions with a business program, is that they are all required, and they are heavily weighted toward economics. For example, as part of those twelve courses, the business student must take Principles of Economics (I and II), Money and Banking, and Business and Economic Statistics and must either complete an economics internship or do independent study. In spite of the fact that there is no option to specialize in any business discipline like marketing or finance, the popularity of the program is evidenced by the fact that 24 percent of the 1988 graduates were business majors.

Students seeking to develop their Great Communicator skills at liberal arts colleges like Nebraska Wesleyan should consider exploring the following courses.

English

Advanced Composition: An advanced course in composition with emphasis upon "utilitarian" forms and techniques. The course deals with various applications of exposition, argument, and persuasion: its aim is to increase the skills of persons for whom English will be an essential professional tool.

Business Writing: An advanced course in composition focusing on modern business writing. The course deals with principles of business writing, style, organization of business messages, audience analysis, and message format. Required writing includes business letters, memoranda, and business reports, one of which is a major analytical report on a contemporary business problem.

Speech Communications and Theater Arts

Fundamentals of Speech: The basic course in effective public speaking. It emphasizes careful preparation and critical thinking as the basis of speech and includes regular classroom speaking and constructive criticism.

Beginning Debate: A course in public speaking emphasizing the study of evidence and organizational strategy.

Organizational Communication: A study of the verbal and nonverbal messages that flow throughout an organization and how they affect and are affected by the environment. A field study is included.

Persuasive Communication: Students study the theory and practice of persuasion. Each student applies these theories by designing and carrying out a campaign to effect community change. The campaign must include public speaking. Class methods include guest experts, role playing, and simulations.

Improvisational Theater (Acting): An acting course with emphasis on the techniques of improvisation, imagination development, and sensitivity training. Provides supervised acting experiences.

Additionally, as mentioned, both business and economics majors at Nebraska Wesleyan are required to complete an internship or field experience. The intent of the internship, according to LaVerne Rudell, head of the business administration and economics department, is "to provide a practical business application experience for the student that may be used on the student's resume, to enhance the student's interviewing and application skills, and to assist a student in career selection and development." The internship requirements are very specific: (1) Each student must find, through an interview, a firm to serve as sponsor and agree to provide a meaningful job experience related to the student's field of study; (2) the student must work a minimum of 9–10 hours per week at the sponsor's business for fifteen weeks; (3) the student must have an evaluation of performance completed by the sponsor and submitted to the intern coordinator at the end of the term; and (4) *the student must complete a major paper at the end of the term, to be evaluated by the intern coordinator.*

It should also be noted that Nebraska Wesleyan has, like some schools, taken the issue of integrating writing skills across business courses quite seriously. For example, long- and short-answer essay examinations, as well as individual term papers, are used in most classes. Group term papers of from ten to fifty pages in length are assigned in Marketing, Advanced Personnel, Organizational Behavior, Small Business Management, Collective Bargaining, and Business Policy.

Writing for the school newspaper at Nebraska Wesleyan and competing on the debate team are also obvious ways to improve communication skills.

Grammar Counts

We hope that we have finally laid to rest one myth. Making statements like "We *was* going to finish that report by Monday," writing "principal" in a report when you meant *principle,* and spelling "a lot" as "alot" do count. In fact, poor writing and speaking skills can undermine months of hard—and thoughtful—work.

Some years ago one of the authors of this book was teaching at a major state university in the Midwest. The class dealt with people skills—how to understand and communicate effectively with other people. Students came from a variety of majors; some were freshmen and others were graduating seniors. They were to maintain a journal as part of the class assignment. One of the most common questions asked about the journal assignment was "Does grammar count?" *Of course it counted.* It would have been a dereliction of the teacher's professional responsibility not to count it, because your grammar skills are continually being evaluated, whether in school, at work, or elsewhere. In fact, as a student, you have a right to demand that *all* your professors provide you with feedback about your writing and communication skills. The feedback may be harsh and painful at first. But the only way to improve your skills is to get honest feedback.

Strong communication skills, in fact, were probably mislabeled when we earlier referred to them as success skills. They are more like survival skills. No matter how *successful* you are in your technical work, you won't *survive* if you cannot articulate your thoughts in clearly written and spoken words.

═══ SNAPSHOTS ═══

William C. Creasy is an expert. In 1982 he left UCLA with a Ph.D. in English and an M.B.A. in marketing to work at Mellon Bank in Pittsburgh as a senior financial analyst. Less than two years later he moved on to become a vice president at First Interstate Bancorp, the nation's seventh-largest bank holding company. After a year as director of retail strategy, he was promoted to managing principal of First Interstate's management consulting company. According to Bill, his quick steps up the corporate ladder resulted from his expertise—but probably not the kind that you may think. "In my experience a person needs four skills to be successful in banking. First, you need technical skills; in my case this meant knowing the mechanics of marketing and financial analysis. Next, you need implementation skills. Corporations are complex organizations, so it's important to know how to work within them to get things done. The other two skills are writing and speaking.

"Frankly, many of my colleagues had better technical skills than I; many even had better ideas. But in every meeting, whether with one person or twenty, I was always prepared. I had identified the central issues we were to discuss, and I had structured what I was going to say and how I was going to say it in a rhetorically effective way. Of course, I would use color slides and computer graphics, but more importantly, I would speak passionately and convincingly about issues that really mattered to the people sitting in the room. Business communications is fundamentally persuasion, and I was always very careful to focus not on what I wanted to say but on achieving the response I wanted from my audience."

In 1988 Bill Creasy returned to UCLA to teach English 131B, an advanced writing course that focuses on the complexities of business and professional writing. The course isn't merely a series of writing assignments; rather, Bill operates his classroom as William C. Creasy & Associates, a private management consulting firm, and his students write all their letters, memos, proposals, and reports in response to problems that arise in a real business environment. He conducts each class as a staff meeting with no-excuses deadlines. And what do Bill's students think? Robert Francais, now working in the Los Angeles office of Deloitte, Haskins and Sells, says, "This kind of class helped me make a successful transition from the academic to the professional world. The skills that I learned in Dr. Creasy's class didn't stay in the classroom. I use them every day."

Whether it's the transition from UCLA to an accounting firm or from Providence College to an advertising agency, the expectations are the same. Grammar, spelling, writing, speaking, and listening—*they all count.*

The other author of this book regularly teaches Introduction to Marketing, a course typically aimed at college juniors. On the first day of class it is standard practice to go over the roster of students who have signed up for the course. It is a time to get to know people. It is also time to enforce the rules. One of the rules that always needs enforcing is the term "junior-level." Inevitably there are several freshmen and sophomores in the room. The question is always the same, "Why are you here?" and the answer also never seems to vary, "Because I'm a marketing major." This statement is accompanied by a set jaw and a confident look. These students think they know their mission; that they are one or two years ahead of schedule merely underscores their determination. But our advice? Don't be in such a rush. Your ability to understand and apply the techniques of business does not occur in a vacuum. Solutions are hardly ever simple; there are always options and complications. It is imperative, therefore, that you invest the time and effort and prepare yourself to read with comprehension, listen intently, question effectively, and write persuasively. These skills and the others that are listed at the head of this chapter set the context for learning. The Great Communicator of today is the person who is preparing himself or herself to solve the real-world business problems of tomorrow.

John Ciardi, in a recent edition of the *Saturday Review,* expresses the thought in more graphic detail: "An Annapolis midshipman taking a course in Spanish wrote that Sancho Panza [Don Quixote's irrepressible sidekick] 'always rode a burrow.' His Spanish professor wrote in the margin: '*Burro* is an ass. *Burrow* is a hole in the ground. As a future Naval officer, you are expected to know the difference.'"

4

The Team Player

Interpersonal Skills Inventory

Able to influence others • Negotiate and compromise • Withstand and resolve conflict • Understand the feelings of others • Encourage debate • Organize and delegate tasks • Motivate and develop other people • Appreciate/reward people's efforts

U.S. businesses are discovering an important new strategy to enhance organizational effectiveness and increase productivity. Corporations across the country are spending millions to help their employees learn about this new tool. Senior managers hope it will radically alter the way corporations and large organizations structure the work environment. Tens of thousands of employees at big and small firms are attending special workshops and weeklong training programs to learn about the theoretical basis and operational dimensions of this new corporate resource. Social scientists based at business schools and sociology departments are building their research careers by studying this new tool.

What is this critical new skill? *Teamwork.* Sound familiar? It is a skill that young boys—and increasingly young girls—learn as participants in school sports programs. Yet corporations are spending millions of dollars to teach—or in many cases reteach—their people about teamwork.

Why is teamwork seen as being novel and innovative? Because many factors have come together to create a kind of antiteamwork culture in U.S. corporations. First, Americans have thought of themselves as rugged individualists. European observers have long characterized Americans as placing a strong value on individualism. This was one of the main observations of Alexis de Tocqueville, a young Frenchman who toured the United States in the early 1800s. His journal of those travels, *Democracy in America*—intended to help explain the young American democracy to European readers—has since become an influential and widely cited classic work in the cultural and political history of the United States.

Second, the early history of U.S. corporations emphasized an authoritarian work environment. Management *told* labor what to do and how to do it; senior managers *told* junior managers what had to be done and often recommended ways to accomplish these tasks. In short, the corporate history of the United States reflects a top-down management orientation: workers, at all levels, were not part of a team; rather, they were treated as employees who required substantial supervision and whose only contribution to corporate goals was the labor they provided for manufacturing new goods.

Finally, and more recently, the 1970s and 1980s seem to have been a period of individual preoccupation with self. Indeed, this preoccupation with self has been captured by author Tom Wolfe, a much published and a very astute social observer perhaps best known to today's college students for his 1988 bestseller, *Bonfire of the Vanities*. Wolfe tagged the 1970s "the Me Decade," calling it "the greatest age of individualism in American history!" Wolfe compared it to a great religious wave, an awakening: "And this one has the mightiest, holiest roll of all, the beat goes . . . *Me* . . . *Me* . . . *Me* . . . *Me*. . . ."

The New Corporate Culture

We seem to value our individualism now just as much as ever. In all walks of life our society continues to emphasize the individual. But there is, at least in the workplace, a new recognition that successful organizations must pull together all their human resources to forge a strong, viable organizational culture that emphasizes teamwork. (See Table 4.)

In recent years, U.S. industry has begun to see just how important the notion of teamwork is to quality and productivity. Indeed, the examples are all around us. More than a decade ago the Swedish car manufacturer Volvo abandoned the traditional automobile manufacturing line, replacing it with mobile platforms for the car chassis; employee teams work on one car section or system at a time. The Volvo approach fosters top-quality products, employee concern for

---

Table 4. The New Corporate Curriculum?

(percentage of companies planning to teach key skills to
employees in the next three years)

Teamwork	39
Problem solving	38
Oral communications	34
Creative thinking	31

Source: Anthony P. Carnevale, Leila J. Gainer, and Ann S. Meltzer, *Workplace Basics: The Skills Employers Want* (American Society for Training and Development and U.S. Department of Labor), 1989, p. 8.

enhancing production, increased productivity, and high employee morale.

Our Japanese competitors have a far better developed sense of teamwork than we do; indeed, it is embedded into their corporate culture. Take, for example, the comments of Konosuke Matsushita, chairman of Matsushita Electric Industrial Company (Panasonic), one of Japan's largest firms. Speaking to a group of U.S. business leaders in 1979, Matsushita offered a stark assessment of the differences between Japanese and American management cultures and the role of teamwork.

> *For us [in Japan], the core of management is precisely this art of mobilizing and pulling together the intellectual resources of all employees in service to the firm. Because we [in Japan] have examined [better than our U.S. counterparts] the scope of the new economic and technological challenges, we know that a handful of technocrats, no matter how brilliant and smart they may be, is no longer enough to [ensure] corporate success.*
>
> *Only by drawing on the combined brainpower of all its employees can a firm face up to the turbulence and constraints of today's environment. That is why [Japan's] large firms give their employees three to four times more training than [U.S. companies]. This is why [Japanese firms] foster within the firm such intensive communications and constantly seek everyone's suggestions, and why they demand from the educational system an increasing number of specialists, as well as bright, well-educated generalists, because these people are the lifeblood of industry.*

In the United States, corporate leaders, senior managers, industrial consultants, and campus-based business school faculty members are giving new attention to teamwork as an important element in corporate culture and an essential skill for successful managers. Bob

Bookman, president of a Washington, D.C., consulting firm, argues strongly for this change: "In essence, I'm suggesting that many people need to change their fundamental work styles today to be successful tomorrow." The teamwork approach, according to Bookman, requires that coworkers shed some of their notions of individualism and accept a different set of philosophies in the workplace.

- *Trust.* Employees and supervisors are typically wary of each other, the greatest obstacle to flexibility and information flow.

- *Involvement.* Teamwork success is dependent on everyone believing his or her participation counts, regardless of where he or she fits into the hierarchy.

- *Point-of-View Communication.* Among America's most popular TV commercials are the Miller Lite ads, which exemplify our cultural ideal of good fellowship. But they always come down to an ambivalence of opinion: "tastes great" versus "less filling." Point-of-view communication doesn't collide like that. People aren't right or wrong. Opinions count as much as facts and figures.

- *Emphasis on Others' Strengths, Not Weaknesses.* Employees must look for ways to complement, rather than compete with, each other.

- *Persuasive—Not Paternalistic—Leadership.* Managers must become good listeners, willing to involve others in decision making. Ask U.S. workers who the boss is, and they all know. Ask Japanese workers the same question, and they point to everyone around them. They all take personal responsibility.

- *Precise Objectives.* Team members need to know precise goals and deadlines in solving defined problems. Otherwise, there is the same effect as an airline pilot telling the passengers, "We're going to *try* to land now."

Corporations across the country, in all states and in all sectors, are beginning to make changes. One example is Xerox Corporation, which has gone so far as to incorporate the team notion into a recent advertising campaign: *Team Xerox.* Why? Because Xerox had little choice if the company was to survive. Xerox has long enjoyed a reputation for technological innovation, with products ranging from copiers to office automation systems (early versions of advanced personal computers with integrated software). Moreover, the organizational model for the Xerox sales force has long stressed teamwork: an account triad consisting of a sales rep working with an account service liaison and a technical support person. Nonetheless, Xerox experienced a steady decline in its share of the worldwide copier market throughout the 1980s. Corporate leaders launched a top-to-bottom recasting of its corporate culture. Xerox executives are counting on "people power" and team spirit to turn the company around.

At Xerox the conversion has relied on an unprecedented training program, undertaken at the expense of short-term earnings. By 1988, all of Xerox's employees will have completed at least 48 hours of schooling in "Leadership Through Quality," a problem-solving system that teaches workers to think of everyone their work affects—whether the next fellow on the assembly line or the purchaser of a $30,000 copier—as a customer to please.

Has Xerox's investment in teamwork been successful? You bet! Following several years of poor corporate performance and missed market opportunities, Xerox won the prestigious Malcolm Baldrige Award in 1989. This award was created by the U.S. Congress to motivate U.S. companies to improve their worldwide competitiveness by improving total quality management.

Similarly, General Motors, also suffering through a period of major market decline and quality control problems, initiated an experimental program to bring teamwork to automobile assembly lines in the United States.

In 1987 GM began a massive education program when the management and workers at GM's plant in Van Nuys, California, went back to school. The corporate-wide transformation to "worker circles" increases worker responsibility by reducing the number of different job categories from nearly 100 to 3 or 4. Teams of six to ten workers and a team leader decide themselves how best to distribute the work equitably, how to design their jobs most effectively, and how to check for the quality of their own work.

This new application of teamwork and "quality circles" in business represents a major change in the notion of primary work units. It has shifted the emphasis away from the individual working alone to the individual as part of a group, *a team with a specific set of shared responsibilities, goals, and values.*

The reasons for these changes are simple. First, people experience a greater sense of belonging when they are given responsibility. Consider the traditional assembly line: ten people lined up doing small, individual, sequential tasks. A quality control person at the end of the line inspects their work. The new teamwork model emphasizes individual and group responsibility for completing the assigned tasks. The ten people work together, as a group, to accomplish their goals. The inspector is eliminated, and people begin to take pride in their jobs—and their teams. Second, problems are more easily identified and solved. The people who are closest to the problems are given the authority, along with the responsibility, to identify and correct those problems. Third, opportunities (new ways of doing things) are a common by-product of groups of people brainstorming or throwing ideas around.

Also, information flow increases substantially as the vertical control of information is replaced by the horizontal coordination of information, that is, as groups of people identify and solve their own problems, eliminating the need for inspectors who would report problems to their superiors. And finally, there is peer learning. Research demonstrates that small groups have a unique self-education process. People within the group who understand a concept or a problem become "smarter" as they explain it to others who do not understand. Those who don't understand, in turn, work harder to become smarter, because their performance reflects on the quality and pride of the group. (See Fig. 6.)

Working in Groups

So industry is spending millions of dollars teaching its employees all about teamwork. Given the benefits just outlined, it seems a wise investment. But at this point you may be asking yourself a simple question: How difficult can teamwork be? Just as you have been reading and writing for years, you have also been "getting along." It seems a natural thing to do. Many people are good at fitting into groups. They are comfortable and confident. They talk. They smile. What else is there?

The problems that small groups often encounter have been the source of significant research among college professors. Here is a short list of some fairly common problems many groups encounter.

- *Personality and Work-Style Differences.* Team members bring a range of individual motivations and work styles to the group. Some people see a project, a job, or a class assignment as just one more of "life's little requirements." Their primary goal is to get it done and move on. For others, the project or task is an important personal statement. They take pride in their contribution. Work styles also differ. Some members are highly structured—meticulous in their approach. Such rigidity can stifle another person, who is more freewheeling. Effective groups have to work through these individual differences that might otherwise affect overall group productivity and performance.

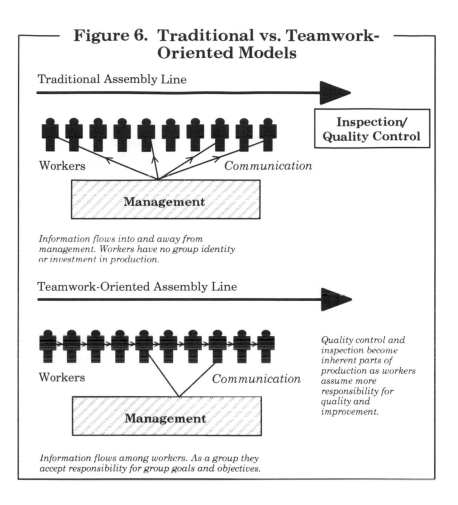

Figure 6. Traditional vs. Teamwork-Oriented Models

Traditional Assembly Line

Inspection/Quality Control

Workers   *Communication*

Management

Information flows into and away from management. Workers have no group identity or investment in production.

Teamwork-Oriented Assembly Line

Quality control and inspection become inherent parts of production as workers assume more responsibility for quality and improvement.

Workers   *Communication*

Management

Information flows among workers. As a group they accept responsibility for group goals and objectives.

- *Poor Task/Problem Definition.* Groups often see their role in terms of problem solving, getting the job done. Additionally, out of any team of six to ten people there are usually several aggressive members. You know the type: They want to win, be first, finish the fastest. And so a few excited members can easily entice an entire group to pursue a quick solution without having adequately identified the real problem.

- *Poor Preparation.* Teams may not know how to use meetings effectively. Loosely structured meetings lead to discussions that can ramble on and on—bull sessions. A lack of focus and direction results in wasted time. Also, if members come to a meeting unprepared to discuss the topic at hand, the result is shared ignorance. There's a lot of head nodding and fingertip drumming, but little real decision making and action.

- *Difficulties in Compromising.* Inflexibility is a common problem in groups. Some members usually come into a discussion with their minds made up. They are not interested in new information; they fail to be good listeners. Their inability to adapt to new information that is being shared by others, coupled with a singular desire to "win the argument," creates a roadblock to success.

- *Lack of Empathy.* Team members can become myopic, viewing a team project only in terms of their own efforts, and fail to see the contributions of other team members. It becomes easy to dismiss problems affecting only other team members—a bad case of flu, personal problems at home, other job responsibilities.

- *Poor Conflict Management.* Most researchers subscribe to the idea that conflict has the potential to be either productive or destructive. Conflict can be helpful if it expands the pool of ideas, helps to clarify issues, and prevents a group from reaching a premature consensus. On the other hand, conflict is detrimental if it becomes personal and leads to infighting that drains the energy of group members. Groups need to learn how to resolve internal conflict in a positive, rather than a destructive, manner.

- *Lack of Cohesiveness.* Cohesion can be defined as the total of all factors influencing members to stay in the group. The most consistent research finding is that cohesiveness, the development of shared common goals and a commitment to understand and help each other, is the most important variable in predicting the ability of groups of people to identify and solve problems.

The Boston Celtics have been the world basketball champions numerous times. Sportswriters and sports fans have frequently commented that Boston didn't necessarily have the most talent in the years they won the league championship. True, the Celtics had good players and a few stars. But they weren't unbeatable. So what made the difference? Celtic pride, their ability *to blend together as a cohesive unit.* Team members were committed, they knew each others' strengths and weaknesses, they brought problems to the surface, and they worked hard at being a team. These abilities, people skills, are basically the same regardless of whether you play for the Celtics, work for a large corporation like General Motors or Xerox, or are employed by a small company with only fifteen employees.

The Business School

Just as a business communications course provides the business school foundation for becoming the Great Communicator, an organizational behavior course is the foundation for becoming the Team Player. (At larger institutions organizational behavior is a separate course, while at smaller ones many of the elements of organizational behavior are covered in Introduction to Management.) The key elements of such a course relate to the interaction between technology, environment, and human behavior in an organizational setting. Specific topics include motivation, morale, social structure, communications, hierarchy, and groups.

Such classes often include both lecturing and the use of group projects to expose students to the processes discussed in both the lecture and the text. The projects can involve a report on a particular company's strategy or the analysis of an industry. One important element is that everyone in the group receives the same grade.

While group projects in organizational behavior are generally regarded as an excellent teaching method, you should be aware of one concern. In a recent study published in the *Organizational Behavior Teaching Review,* researchers found that the value of group projects in organizational behavior was diminished by students' concerns over grades. Students tend to compare their own success in classroom activities with that of other students. In their view, competition, not cooperation, paves the road to success. The notion that all members of a group receive the same grade is difficult for students to understand; in fact, students held negative associations with group projects, which might hurt an individual's grade point average (GPA). Many of the better students are simply not willing to risk the uncertainty of working in a group, possibly jeopardizing their GPA. In short, U.S. college students are focused on *me,* as opposed to *we.*

Business communications courses, discussed in the previous chapter, are also good places to develop interpersonal skills. One of the most common tasks in such a class is a group writing assignment. Another useful course is collective bargaining, which requires students to learn about the art of negotiation, persuasion, and compromise. And marketing research courses often place students in teams and then require them to complete a research project involving survey development, customer interviews, and library research. These incremental steps lead to the preparation of a final report, often for a real-world company.

Finally, computer-based simulation exercises and models, which have become increasingly popular in the past decade, provide another opportunity for teamwork training. A marketing simulation, for example, may require that students run a company and make critical choices about new products: pricing (what do we need to make a profit?), advertising (how do we best promote this new product to potential buyers?), and production (how many do we manufacture?). Several such companies compete with each other in an industry and go through a cycle of decision making, for which computer-generated results are produced for analysis and input into the next round of decisions. Simulations have been developed for a wide range of classes in a business college, and they are almost always assigned as a team exercise. Again, cohesiveness—the ability to function together as a single unit—is essential.

And if you still think individual "smarts" are the only factor in being successful, we need to share with you one more research result. Professors at the University of Nevada, Las Vegas, used a business simulation game to study a hypothesis that decision-making groups composed of members who were technically competent but personally incompatible would perform better than groups composed of less technically competent but personally compatible members. The results were striking.

> *Given the high degree of academic and quantitative backgrounds of the members of Team One (the technically competent but interpersonally incompatible group), it would be expected that superior performance would prevail. While there may have been other accompanying factors that were overlooked, it would appear that the reasons for the average performance by Team One were due to the relative inability of one or two hostile people to work together on a cooperative basis.*

In sum, smarts usually will not overcome the basic inability to get along.

The hunt for interpersonal, or team player, skills needs to be exhaustive. The reason is simple. One section of Porter and McKibbin's study of management education, discussed earlier, concerned the amount of emphasis given to *people* versus *technical* skills in the business school curriculum. The differences between the collegiate view of business needs and industry's own perceptions are revealing. (See Table 5.) Clearly, business schools are still not people oriented enough for the business world. The authors of the study conclude that as businesses become less hierarchical, the importance of different relationships begins to emerge. Specifically, lateral relationships (working with people and groups at the same level) are becoming at least as important as the traditional superior/subordinate vertical relationships. They add that "organizations are becoming, on average, more participative with diminished reliance on the exercise of 'top down' autocratic authority. Such tendencies, which probably

Table 5. Perspectives on "People Skill Training" in the Business School Curriculum
(percentages)

	Deans	Faculty	Alumni[a]	CEOs[b]	VPHRs[c]
Too much	11	17	6	9	7
About right	68	60	48	24	21
Too little	21	23	46	67	72

[a]Recent undergraduate business school graduates.
[b]Chief executive officers.
[c]Vice presidents of human resources or the chief personnel officers.

Source: Lyman W. Porter and Lawrence E. McKibbin, *Management Education and Development: Drift or Thrust into the 21st Century* (New York: McGraw-Hill), 1988.

become accentuated in service organizations, have the effect of increasing the need for effective 'soft' (i.e., people) skills even more than has been the case in the past."

So where else in college can the Team Player get experience? We feel that sociology and, again, communications and theater can offer a business student many useful tools for advancing his or her teamwork skills.

Sociology/Psychology

Sociology is concerned with the characteristics, changes, causes, and consequences of group life. Most of the course work in sociology can be divided into two broad categories: macro and micro. The first category deals with societal issues, culture, norms, morality, and policy formation. Many of the introductory courses in sociology stress a macro approach to social issues.

Most of the more advanced courses, however, are micro in orientation and deal with the sociology of the family or other smaller social units. There is much to be learned from this area of sociology. A typical young manager will spend *at least* 8 hours a day on the job. That is more time than he or she spends at home in family activities during the week. While the nature of the problems may change, the fact is that both groups are similar. Both units have hopes and dreams, both have squabbles, bickering, and hurt feelings. Much of business is sociology in action. A business student could greatly improve his or her understanding and appreciation for interpersonal relations by taking a course in group processes or group dynamics in sociology. Such courses emphasize the processes of interaction, dialogue, and conflict in a small-group setting.

Another course that is quite similar is a class in social psychology. It usually discusses attitudes, perceptions, social influence, aggression and helping, and interpersonal relationships. (At many institutions social psychology is offered through the psychology department.)

The Man from Mars

If it were possible for the overworked hypothetical man from Mars to take a fresh view of the people of Earth, he would probably be impressed by the amount of time they spend doing things together in groups. He would note that most people cluster into relatively small groups, with the members residing together in the same dwelling, satisfying their biological needs within the group, depending upon the same source for economic support, rearing children, and mutually caring for the health of one another. He would observe that the education and socialization of children tend to occur in other, usually larger, groups in churches, schools, or other social institutions. He would see that much of the work of the world is carried out by people who perform their activities in close interdependence within relatively enduring associations. He would perhaps be saddened to find groups of men engaged in warfare, gaining courage and morale from pride in their unit and a knowledge that they can depend upon their buddies. He might be gladdened to see groups of people enjoying themselves in recreations and sports of various kinds. Finally he might be puzzled why so many people spend so much time in little groups talking, planning, and being "in conference." Surely he would conclude that if he wanted to understand much about what is happening on Earth he would have to examine rather carefully the ways in which groups form, function and dissolve.

Source: Excerpt from *Group Dynamics: Theory and Research*, 3rd ed., by Dorwin Cartwright and Alvin Zander. Copyright © 1968 by Dorwin Cartwright and Alvin Zander. Reprinted by permission of HarperCollins Publishers, Inc.

Communications

Much of the course work in communications centers on individual skills, for example, public speaking, argumentation, and debate, and on mass communications, which deals with the electronic media. At some institutions, however, there is a specific interpersonal relations course. This course focuses on the dynamics of human interactions in all types of settings. Virtually all of the tools and techniques that a student learns in such a course can be applied to the business world: customer-client relations, team member interactions, and the superior-subordinate relationship.

Theater

In our discussion of communication skills we said that acting courses are useful in establishing a "stage presence." There is another theater activity, however, that is equally important to the skill acquisition process. Every successful theatrical production is a performance that requires the coordination of a diverse group of activities and people. There are the staging and the scenery. There are lighting, sound, and music. There are the lead actors and the supporting cast. A great acting job with poor lighting or sound results in a mediocre performance. Everything must come together once the curtain goes up.

Does this sound familiar? Products or services with a missing part are not going to be wonderfully successful. A car doesn't sell if it is mechanically superior but has poor styling. A bank isn't profitable if it is good at attracting deposits but then makes a host of bad loan decisions. Everything must come together. Such coordination does not just simply happen. It is a natural result of strong interpersonal skills among the key members of work, or production, teams. (For an example of how theater experience translates to the business world, see the Snapshot on page 74.)

Campus Profile
University of California at Berkeley

The University of California at Berkeley is far removed from the quiet confines of Nebraska Wesleyan's Midwest campus. While Nebraska Wesleyan's 1,200 students enjoy close relationships with faculty members, UC Berkeley is a city in itself, with 24 libraries, 100 majors, 5,000 courses, and 22,000 undergraduates. The undergraduate business major at Berkeley is a two-year program that begins in the junior year; graduates receive a Bachelor of Science in Business degree. Students are admitted into the undergraduate business program after completing Berkeley's general education requirements in such

=========== SNAPSHOTS ===========

IBM has a certain image. Most people see it as a company filled with managers (both men and women) wearing dull dark-blue suits. It takes a certain type of person to succeed in the IBM environment. Stephen Baumann, however, is not a typical IBMer.

Steve earned a degree in political science and management from Gettysburg College. Since he has been working in IBM's ROLM Systems Division, however, his success—four promotions and IBM's prestigious National Means Service Award—has been fueled largely by another college passion, the theater: "I began doing musicals in high school—singing, dancing, working the lights. In college I took as many acting and dancing classes as I could squeeze into my schedule. I directed and choreographed a couple of musicals. During the summer I would do summer stock theater in New England. I certainly didn't get involved in theater because I thought it would help a business career. I was doing it all along because it was very rewarding and fun."

Steve's first job after college *was not* with IBM. Rather, he made it to Broadway in the hit musical *A Chorus Line*. After almost a decade in the entertainment business, Steve made a major career shift that brought him to IBM. He is now a telecommunications systems designer: He designs and customizes large telephone systems for corporate clients of ROLM, IBM's telecommunications subsidiary. Steve says that the process can be a time-consuming nightmare for his clients, in part because customers often have too many choices: "Once an organization has purchased one of our systems, I configure the software. That means that I need to coordinate three things: what each department or person wants the phones to do, what features and capabilities the software allows, and how much the organization wants to spend. If everyone wants everything, it can get expensive, so it usually involves a series of trade-offs. After making initial presentations to show people the features, I spend the rest of my time at a company going back and forth, making change after change. There is no easy way to do it. It's a messy job pulling together the details of a million-dollar phone system. But by the end, the process is just like putting on a Broadway show. On the day when the system is turned on, everything better come together or the customer can get pretty hostile."

areas as sociology, history, and biology. Additionally, prospective business majors must also complete seven prerequisite courses before gaining admission into the business program: accounting (introduction), computer science (introduction to programming), economics (introduction), English (reading and composition), mathematics (typically calculus), statistics, and foreign language.

Once admitted to the business school, Berkeley's 550 undergraduate business majors complete a required sequence of core courses. These include Microeconomic Analysis for Business, Macroeconomics for Business, Managerial Accounting, Financial Management, Organizational Behavior, Marketing, and Social and Political Environment of Business. After meeting these core requirements (in their junior year), students concentrate their studies in one of seven fields, for example, accounting, finance, information systems, or real estate. These concentrations, according to Cristina Banks, undergraduate program director, constitute an "intensive curriculum," including economic analysis and policy, finance, marketing, operations management, organizational behavior and industrial relations, real estate, and urban land economics.

Becoming a Team Player at Berkeley or other large universities is just a matter of searching through the course catalog. The search is definitely well worth the time.

Business

Organizational Behavior: A general descriptive and analytical study of organizations from the behavioral science point of view. Problems of motivation, leadership, morale, social structure, groups, communications, hierarchy, and control in complex organizations. The interaction between technology, environment, and human behavior.

Sociology/Psychology

Interpersonal Behavior in Small Groups: An examination of sociological theories and research on behavior in small groups. Topics such as status relations, communication, coalitions, and interpersonal conflict are examined in light of field and laboratory research.

Social Psychology: An examination of major theoretical approaches in social psychology. The approaches may include: symbolic interactionism, neo-behaviorism, psychodynamic analyses, cognitive theories, interpersonal processes, and theories of exchange.

Personality and Social Structure: An analysis of the establishment and growth of personality and of varieties of personality, as a consequence of social experience and an evaluation of socio-psychological and sociological explanations of these developments.

Industrial-Organizational Psychology: Introduction to the field of organizational psychology, covering fundamental theory and concepts in personnel and social aspects in the field. Concerned with the processes involved in developing and maintaining organizations.

Dramatic Arts

The University Theatre: Under the direction of the Department of Dramatic Arts, The University Theatre offers a workshop series of play productions extending into the laboratory of stage practice, the theories of dramatic literature, criticism, and production studied in the departmental curriculum. These programs are selected to present distinguished dramas of various periods and cultures to the university community.

Breaking Chimneys

The notion of teamwork is particularly appropriate for a book intended for college students. Freshman orientation programs, pep rallies, cheerleader-led basketball games, and fraternity and sorority initiations are all group activities. School spirit, or the lack of it, is evident from almost the first day you walk onto a college campus—Go Team! Interestingly, U.S. companies are discovering that teams may also be the productivity breakthrough of the 1990s. A recent survey of almost 500 of the major corporations in the United States by the American Productivity Center in Houston shows that while only 7 percent of the work force is organized into "quality circle" or "self-managed" teams, half the companies questioned say they will be relying significantly more on such teams in the years ahead.

Why? Because, as we have seen, companies that use smaller groups involving from three to twenty-five workers—sometimes blue-collar, sometimes white-collar, sometimes both—usually see productivity rise dramatically. Teams composed of people with different skills, from different parts of the company, can swoop around bureaucratic roadblocks and break down the walls separating different functions to get a job done. As Jerry Junkins, CEO of Texas Instruments, says: "No matter what your business, these teams are the wave of the future."

Although all the examples used in this chapter put a premium on Team Player skills, we need to end with a note of caution. While teamwork may be the wave of the future, according to Jerry Junkins and many others, it is *not a generally accepted organizational practice of today.* The Rubbermaid example (highlighted on the next page) is the exception, not the rule. Most organizations are strict hierarchies. A small group of people have a boss. A small group of bosses have a bigger boss. And so it goes, right on up to the president of the

The Rubbermaid Way

In 1987, Rubbermaid began to develop a so-called auto office, a plastic, portable device that straps onto a car seat; it holds files, pens, and other articles and provides a writing surface. The company assembled a cross-functional team composed of, among others, engineers, designers, and marketers, who together went into the field to ask customers what features they wanted. Says Rubbermaid vice president Lud Huck: "A designer, an engineer, and a marketer all approach research from a different point of view." Huck explains that while a marketer might ask potential customers about price, he'd never think to ask important design questions. With contributions from several different functions, Rubbermaid brought the new product to market last year. Sales are running 50 percent above projections.

Source: Brian Dumaine, "Who Needs a Boss?" *Fortune,* May 7, 1990.

company. Greater pay and power come from progressing up this narrow chimney. Each boss has a vested interest in the chimney. Each has worked long and hard to build it.

Within such a hierarchy, a person with a "cross-functional" problem—say, how to resolve a design problem between engineering and manufacturing—would need to shoot a memo up three layers to the appropriate engineering vice president. That vice president tosses the problem to the vice president of manufacturing, who then kicks it down to the person in the manufacturing area who knows the answer. Then it's back up and down the chimney again. It's a time-consuming process. It's exhausting. But most companies operate this way.

It will be your role in the future to help change the way organizations operate. Don't fall victim to trying to "boss" people, to maintaining control and furthering the inefficiencies that have cost U.S. industry so dearly in the past few decades. Empower the people. Make them responsible for building quality into the product or service, and give them the authority to work together to solve problems. Be a chimney breaker, not a chimney builder.

5

The Technology Master

Technology Skills Inventory

Be familiar with major hardware components • Be able to use
software packages • Use information to aid problem solving • Make
graphic presentations • Access information from many
sources • Be able to transform raw data into useful information •
Analyze data • Communicate using electronic means

The Information Age is now. At least that's the proclamation of dozens of recent books intended for business professionals. "Technology is . . . a wild card affecting every aspect of doing business," writes management consultant Tom Peters in *Thriving on Chaos*. Indeed, almost anything and everything you read these days about the future of U.S. (and international) business emphasizes the key role of technology in business activities and the dramatic transition from *manufacturing products* to *managing information*. Some examples:

- The "shift in strategic resources from an industrial to an information society" is one of the ten major forces that are helping to "reinvent" the corporation, according to John Naisbitt and Patricia Aburdene, authors of the 1988 bestseller *Reinventing the Corporation*.

- "Information is the new transforming resource of society," writes Leon Martel, management consultant and author of *Mastering Change*. "Today information is rapidly replacing energy as society's main transforming resource. . . . But information is more than just a new, more powerful transforming resource. It has qualities that set it apart from the transforming qualities of the natural power and created energy it is replacing. Natural power is limited; and created energy is finite and expendable. But information is not used up and does not disappear. It is always available, to be called on again and again: and for this reason, it continues to accumulate, becoming an ever increasing resource."

- "What the invention of the printing press did for mankind five centuries ago, the computer is doing today. It has spurred a radical change in every aspect of our lives, moving with devastating speed . . . ," observes French writer and social critic Jean-Jacques Servan-Schreiber in his 1986 book, *The Knowledge Revolution.*

This transition to the Information Age has been reflected in many new products over the past decade. The most important of these products, of course, is the personal computer. The first personal computers (or microcomputers), such as the Altair and Apple II, were introduced in the mid and late 1970s. They were targeted primarily for hobbyists and computer hackers. However, productivity software, such as speadsheets and word processing packages, soon made these machines very useful and powerful tools that quickly gained popularity in the business market.

Apple's marketing promotion for the 1984 Macintosh product launch talked about a target market of some 15 million "knowledge workers" based in corporations, small businesses, science labs, and colleges and universities. Yet Apple's numbers badly underestimated the real number of knowledge workers in the United States in the mid 1980s. Harlan Cleveland, director of the Hubert H. Humphrey Institute of Public Affairs at the University of Minnesota, observes we have experienced a dramatic shift toward jobs that involve "information work."

In 1920, fewer than 10 percent of the American workers were doing information work. In the United States, still the most developed postindustrial country, more than half of all work, as defined by the Census Bureau's employment categories, is now information work—not only writing and calculating but also what executives, salespeople, advertisers, lawyers, accountants, secretaries, programmers, consultants, and hundreds of other kinds of workers do.

The Census Bureau doesn't admit it, but it seems likely that the ratio of brainwork to drudgery keeps rising in nearly every job. Many tasks are still comparatively routine, of course; but any routine that can be taken over by a machine will be lost to the labor force. A machine is a slave, and free people won't indefinitely opt to compete with slaves for their jobs.

In this picture the actual production, extraction, and growing of things now soaks up less than a quarter of our human resources. Of all the rest, which used to be lumped together as "services," more than two-thirds are information workers. By the end of the century, more than two-thirds of the whole labor force will be information workers. [original emphasis]

Cleveland's assessments reflect the trends shown in Table 6. A century ago, half of all U.S. workers (virtually all males) were involved in either farming or mining, while a third worked in manufacturing and commerce. Service jobs accounted for just one eighth of the work force in 1880, and information work required the skills of only 2 of every 100 workers. By 1975, however, service jobs (involving both men and women) accounted for 17 percent of the work force. Information work grew by a factor of 25, to account for fully half of the work force. Knowledgeable authorities estimate that information and service jobs will account for two thirds to three fourths of the jobs in the U.S. work force by the end of this decade.

The labor force trends shown in Table 6 reflect the fundamental changes in the United States and the rest of the developed world over the past two centuries. The Agrarian Revolution lasted for thousands of years, roughly up to the middle of the eighteenth century. The Industrial Revolution, which lasted for nearly two centuries, marked

Table 6. U.S. Work Force Distribution, 1880–2000

(percentages)

	1880	1920	1955	1975	2000 (est.)
Agriculture and extraction (e.g., mining)	50	28	14	4	2
Manufacturing, commerce, and industry	36	53	37	29	22
Other services	12	10	20	17	10
Information, knowledge, and education	2	9	29	50	66

Source: G. Molitor, Public Policy Forecasting, Inc.

the end of farming as the primary form of labor in the developed world. Currently the Information Revolution of the closing years of the twentieth century signals the end of manufacturing as the primary form of work activity. These changes represent fantastic shifts in the allocation of labor, the description of work, and the definition of jobs.

These structural changes in the work force have been linked to the key symbols of their respective eras by management consultant Jeffrey Hallett. Hallett's chart (see Table 7) moves us through the dominant technologies of these periods (from plow to machine to computer), identifies the key energy sources of the era (animal, fossil fuel, or mind power), and defines both the organizational forms and the production needs of the age. The differences across the three eras—agricultural, manufacturing (or industrial), and information—are striking.

Table 7. Fundamental Changes in the Transition from an Agricultural to an Information Society

Model	Agriculture (to the 1800s)	Manufacturing (1800–1980s)	Information (1980s —>)
Dominant technology	Plow	Machine	Computer
Science	Civil engineering	Mechanical engineering	Bioengineering
Goal	Survival	Material wealth	Personal growth
Output	Food	Goods	Information
Strategic resource	Land	Capital	Knowledge
Organizational form	Family	Corporation	Networks
Energy source	Animal	Fossil fuel	Mind
Primary work	Farmer	Laborer	Entrepreneur
Nature of production	Self	Mass	Individualized

Source: Jeffrey J. Hallett, *Worklife Visions,* American Society for Personnel Administration, Alexandria, Virginia, 1987, p. 23.

The Age of Technology

Most historians of computing agree that the so-called computer age began in February 1946, with the public dedication of ENIAC, the first digital computer. By current standards, ENIAC was a primitive monster: It had some 18,000 vacuum tubes and covered roughly 1,800 square feet (approximately the size of a small house). The machines that followed ENIAC in the first years of the computer age were designed generally for scientific purposes, to "crunch numbers" for government agencies like the Census Bureau and the Department of Defense. The commercial market for computers did not exist; indeed, a late 1940s internal market assessment at IBM (then a large manufacturer of calculating machines) speculated that the total worldwide market for the commercial computers (that is, business use of computing machines) would probably not exceed perhaps six or a dozen machines annually.

How things have changed. The IBM PC, Macintosh, or PC clone desktop computer you routinely used in high school and now use in college is far more powerful than the computers that cost hundreds of thousands of dollars as recently as ten or fifteen years ago. Analysts note that if the automobile industry had experienced over the past thirty years the rate of change under way in the computer industry, everyone would be driving a Rolls-Royce that cost only a few thousand dollars and got 100-plus miles to the gallon. Computer costs have declined dramatically, while power and access have increased significantly. In short, computers have changed dramatically—and so have the people who use them.

As recently as a decade ago there was but one fundamental computing skill: programming. Computer users were computer programmers. People who needed the computational power of computers for statistical, financial, data, or accounting and inventory analysis depended on a core group of computer professionals who were the real computer users. The systems operators and programmers really used the machine. The computer operators and systems analysts were the priests of technology: only they understood the computer, and only they could master the difficult and arcane jargon that got the machine to churn lots of data into potentially useful information.

Yet in just one decade, the 1980s, our understanding of the role of the computer changed dramatically. Hundreds of thousands of people who never thought of themselves as "computer types" now feel that they are nonetheless very skilled computer users. Moreover, they have come to depend on their desktop computer—and would never, ever part with it. Writers, journalists, product designers, artists, accountants, small-business owners, marketing professionals, tax specialists, architects, and teachers are examples of those whose jobs, although not traditionally viewed as high-computer-use careers, have become almost computer dependent.

Corporate Computing

The 1950s saw the first movement of computers into corporations. Companies discovered that computers could do a very good job of managing repetitive tasks, such as preparing invoices. The 1960s and 1970s saw the explosive growth of computing in large and medium-sized businesses as computers evolved into more flexible resources capable of performing a rich array of tasks (and became available at a wide range of prices).

Yet the greatest and most dramatic changes in corporate computing occurred in the past decade. At the beginning of the 1980s the computer was a key resource, but one managed, as we have noted, by an elite group of technical specialists—programmers and systems analysts. Today, however, the personal computer has become a ubiquitous resource, ever present on the desks of secretaries, managers, sales personnel, marketing representatives, and senior executives. True, the technological elite still controls the mainframe and minicomputers that are kept behind closed doors, the big machines handling the company payroll, accounts receivable and payable, personnel, inventory, and dozens of corporate-wide data-intensive activities. They manage the technology at the heart of any corporation's information system.

But big corporations and small businesses also have high expectations of their desktop computers—and the people who use them. The key word here is *productivity*. Increasing competitiveness—the pressure to produce more goods or services at lower cost—requires that firms, both large and small, find ways to enhance productivity and increase employee effectiveness. In many cases, computers are the resource that permits firms to do both. No question—computers *are* replacing people in many organizations. Some examples:

- *Secretarial Services.* Years ago, middle-level managers and senior executives had their own secretaries and would not have been seen anywhere near a typewriter. Typing was (and remains) a low-status clerical skill, a task assigned to secretaries. But today, of course, a growing number of small businesses and large corporations expect their managers and executives to be comfortable with computer keyboards and to accomplish a wide range of tasks, such as preparing memos and drafting reports and proposals, that were formerly performed by secretaries.

Additionally, many firms have reduced their clerical staffs, for example, people in the typing pool, because of the increased productivity provided by desktop computers used for word processing. (See the feature on keyboarding on page 86.)

- *Accounting.* Hundreds of thousands of small businesses save tens of thousands of dollars each year because they have moved their accounting work off the desk of the company bookkeeper or accountant and into the hard disk of a desktop computer. A modest investment in accounting software helps many small businesses and start-up firms take control of their financial paperwork and resources. Rather than employ an in-house accountant, they can hire a CPA to drop in for a few days each month. This contributes to increased productivity and helps to reduce costs.

- *Electronic Mail.* Computers are the backbone of a new kind of instantaneous, low-cost information service that is increasingly common in both large and small organizations: *electronic mail.* I can send a memo or a budget model from my desk to your desk, across the office or across the country, in a matter of seconds. I am no longer dependent on the company mail room, the U.S. Postal Service, or a private courier service, such as Federal Express, to get important materials and short messages from my desk to other people.

- *Graphics and Printing.* Most people do not think of themselves as artists and graphic designers. However, the drawing tools pioneered on the Macintosh and increasingly available on all kinds of personal computers permit almost anyone to create reasonable—indeed, impressive—graphics in very little time. Managers, sales representatives, and senior executives can produce their own graphics in an hour, rather than sending a job over to an in-house art department or out to an art firm or graphics consultant. Art and printing departments can do complex layouts in hours instead of days.

- *Information Access.* In some companies, information is a very hot commodity. Managers need up-to-date information—*and they need it now.* Today one researcher with a personal computer and a modem can tap into a rich array of electronic information resources that in the past would occupy a small army of research staffers plowing through paper, magazines, books, financial reports, and journals.

How Typing Became Keyboarding

Several studies of office automation in the early 1980s identified a major barrier to executive productivity: the absence of *typing skills* among middle-level and senior executives. If you could not type, you could not use a computer.

This created a major dilemma for many businesses and senior executives. Typing was a low-status clerical task. Indeed, many male managers often took great pride in the fact that they could not type, viewing typing as a "woman's job." (Their girlfriends or wives typed their papers while they were in college and grad school; their secretaries typed their office papers.)

You can quickly see the problem. Low-status typing skills were the gateway to a high-status computer. The task: Convince a largely male population with high-status job aspirations that low-status skills are essential to their job performance and future job security.

The solution: Office automation experts succeeded in converting *typing*, a low-status *clerical* task, into *keyboarding*, a high-status *computer* activity. Male middle-managers may not like it any better, but the semantic spin makes it easier to handle. Telling associates that you've been taking computer and keyboarding lessons is more palatable than saying you've been going to typing classes.

All this may seem routine and even commonplace if you've been using desktop computers since you were 13 or 14. But it can be very threatening to many very successful business managers and sales reps. Who is most threatened by the growing corporate use of computers in sales offices and the executive suite? Male middle-managers in their late thirties, forties, and fifties. For many people in this group, the computer may represent a threat both to their jobs and to their self-esteem. They remember the computer as the tool of the techies, and they remember typing—the most basic computer skill—as something they consciously avoided during high school and college. At 38 or 47 or 55 these men often find it difficult (and frequently embarrassing) to acquire what they view as a low-status skill. And they may be uncomfortable asking younger people and subordinates for technical assistance on the small points of spreadsheet formulas, graphic layouts, or database management on a PC; it upsets the self-image of a self-reliant business professional. But they do not have an option. As futurists and management consultants John Naisbitt and Patricia

Aburdene report, technological innovation has major consequences for middle-aged middle-managers.

Self-management is replacing staff managers who manage people; the computer is replacing line managers who manage systems.

What really enables [organizations] to shrink middle management is the computer, which gives top management the information previously obtained from middle managers.

And although many executives resist typing on their keyboards, computers are most definitely finding their way into the executive suite. . . . Now with the computer to keep track of information and people, middle managers are seen as disposable. . . .

Today, computers are replacing middle managers at a much greater rate than robots are replacing assembly line workers. . . . Once indispensable to senior executives, many middle managers are now watching computers do their job in a fraction of the time and at a percentage of the cost.

In short, almost every business, large or small, has come to view the *new technologies* of the 1980s as *key technologies* for the 1990s. The increasingly competitive environment of the 1990s and the twenty-first century will require that all businesses make every effort to use technology to enhance productivity and control costs.

14,000 Square Feet for Computers at the University of Michigan

Humanities students who wanted to use computers at the University of Michigan once had to go to one of the thirty public sites in academic buildings and dormitories. Now, however, they have what may be the largest university computer room in the country. It's a 14,000-square-foot space that holds 260 Apple Macintosh computers and 70 IBM PCs and will be able to accommodate the 30 more workstations that are in this year's budget.

The space was created by combining two classrooms and a courtyard that links Angell, Haven, and Mason halls, the main humanities classroom buildings. The renovation, including skylights to enclose the courtyard, cost $2.8 million. The computers, software, and furniture cost an additional $1.5 million, university officials say. Michigan has more than 15,000 computers and workstations, more than 2,000 of them available in public sites.

Source: The Chronicle of Higher Education, March 10, 1990, p. A22.

Campus Computing

Campus computing actually predates corporate computing. The original research that ultimately led to the development of the computer was done on college campuses during and just after World War II. Moreover, scientific researchers saw applications for computers long before corporations recognized their value for manipulating large amounts of data.

Colleges and universities were also particularly enamored of the computer as a teaching machine. For almost three decades, beginning in the mid 1960s, many campus researchers and educators have been candid about their great, if only sometimes fulfilled, hopes for using the computer to enhance instruction and learning.

Schools and colleges were very visible participants in the decade-long movement toward microcomputers or desktop computers that began in the late 1970s. Early in the 1980s, as elementary and high schools began to dabble in the area of computer literacy, most efforts focused on traditional technical skills, the bits, bytes, and BASIC approach to computing. Today, however, most efforts emphasize application skills rather than technical skills, that is, word processing, spreadsheets, and graphics over programming.

Colleges and corporations across the country have been purchasing microcomputers or desktop computers—IBM PCs, PC clones, and Macintosh systems—by the dozens, hundreds, and thousands since the mid 1980s. Small colleges have come to view microcomputers (or desktop computers) as a comparatively inexpensive way to provide computer resources they could not afford in the past. And some large campuses have purchased hundreds or even thousands of desktop computers. Whereas a decade ago computer labs were limited largely to the physical sciences, computer science, statistically oriented social sciences, and business programs, today you can find computer labs almost anywhere on campus, including the English, art, and music departments. In short, computing is a fundamental component of the college experience in the 1990s. (See the story of the University of Michigan on page 87.)

These changes in computing parallel the expectations of college students. Upwards of 60 percent of the nation's college freshmen report that they had some type of computing class in high school; almost a third identify themselves as frequent PC users. Additionally, in fall 1989 better than one eighth of the nation's college freshmen indicated that they planned to buy a personal computer before the end of their first year in college. The campus investment in computing reflects in part an awareness that computing skills are valuable for students in all majors and are essential skills in the job

SNAPSHOTS

What image comes to mind when you think of someone who is a technology master? Be honest: You probably think of a male science major, someone who looks like the stereotypical nerd in TV programs and Hollywood movies: tall, thin, smart, glasses, interested only in science and computers, not very good at sports, and not very comfortable with adults or the opposite sex.

Enter Terri St. Cyr, an attractive, bright, energetic, athletic UCLA graduate who was an undergraduate French major. Although her career path took a few turns in the first years after graduation, Terri has spent the past five years helping both college administrators and corporate officials learn about technology and desktop computers.

Terri is the absolute opposite of the hacker stereotype. But what's a French major doing messing around with technology and teaching corporate executives, many of them trained engineers, how to use desktop computers? Terri's experience suggests that there are many routes to becoming a Technology Master.

"During my last year at UCLA I had a part-time job at a research institute on campus. This group was one of the first at UCLA to use desktop computers. I initially learned about desktops using an Apple III [a product made obsolete by the IBM PC and Apple Macintosh]. My introduction to a PC was through word processing. I also learned how to use spreadsheet, graphics, and database software.

"When I finished my degree at UCLA I was not sure what I wanted to do. I confronted the classic dilemma that many humanities majors experience after they graduate: What can I do with my degree in French language and literature? After some careful career exploration, I finally decided to become a physical therapist. So I continued to work at the research institute while I took extra courses to prepare for a master's program in physical therapy. Well, this was now 1984 [the year Apple announced the Macintosh and three years after the IBM PC was born]. The UCLA researchers were just gearing up on a few new projects that would help college administrators learn about computers. I got involved in several workshop training sessions and ultimately assumed responsibility for coordinating these programs and running certain parts of the training. The more training I did, the more I began to rethink my earlier plans about the physical therapy program.

"I stayed at UCLA for a few more years, ultimately assuming some managerial responsibilities on a major project involved with training college administrators how to use PCs. That experience, training people to use PCs, has served me well. I have no regrets about my years studying French literature at UCLA. However, there is no question in my mind that I got my current job at Rockwell International because of my work experience with computers while I was going to school."

market. Indeed, some observers (we are among them) believe campuses have a responsibility to help their students acquire these now essential skills.

The Six Basic Computer Skills

So how do you become conversant with the technology that is increasingly available on college campuses and increasingly *required* in large firms and small businesses? We recommend that you become a Technology Master. Today's Technology Master is not necessarily a programmer, but someone like Terri St. Cyr, who understands the value of the new technologies and, as a first step, has mastered the six basic computing skills. These are essential skills for today's college students and tomorrow's business leaders.

Word Processing

Everyone writes. And word processing is a fundamental computer skill for *every* college student and every future manager. Regardless of your specialization or major, throughout your career you will have to write—reports, memoranda, letters, proposals, and so on. And the same writing skills that you use in college for term papers and special projects will help you in the job market. The marketing professional, for example, will need to submit plans for a product promotion strategy. The accountant will have to summarize a site audit for a client in clear, concise language. Sales managers routinely prepare proposals for clients and reports for the home office.

Forget the old (and very expensive) situation, in which secretaries transcribed dictation or deciphered handwritten notes. Today's corporations and small businesses are trying to run lean and mean, with fewer support staff. Consequently, you will have to be self-sufficient in preparing much of your written work.

Financial Analysis (Spreadsheets)

The spreadsheet (products like Lotus 1-2-3, Microsoft's Excel, or Informix's WingZ) helped move the microcomputer out of the hands of programmers and into the hands of financial analysts, corporate managers, sales representatives, and the vast numbers of nontechnical people who need a powerful analytical tool. The most important benefit of spreadsheets is the capability gained for doing quick computations and what-if analysis. You can build a budget and then run variations on your budget model, focusing on the costs and consequences of various changes in your model. For example, if I know the basic relationship between price and sales revenues, a spreadsheet allows me to look at the effect on a balance sheet. How might revenue change if I increase prices by 3 percent or by 5 percent? What if I charge $4.95? What if personnel expenditures drop by 3.4 percent annually over four years? Repetitive as well as complex financial calculations are made simple by a spreadsheet.

Graphics

A picture *is* worth a thousand words. Computer-generated data graphs, via screen or on paper as handouts, have emerged in recent years as an essential tool for many people in business. This skill will be even more important in the 1990s. One person working at one computer for an hour or two can produce the kinds of graphic-rich presentation materials that used to occupy a department of graphic designers for several days. Computers make it easy to prepare customized, professional-looking presentation materials.

Desktop computers quickly generate a wide array of "pictures"—data charts and schematic graphics. For example, many of the figures and all of the graphs presented in this book were originally created by the authors with a desktop computer. Data graphs give life and meaning to numerical data; schematic graphics help show relationships among organizations or concepts that may be difficult to express in words. At the least, graphics enrich reports and presentations, making concepts and data more accessible and better understood. In sum, be prepared to create your own pictures.

Database Management

Managers manage information—about people, places, products, and finances. Consequently, managers must be familiar with different approaches to data management—on desktop computers and on mainframe systems. Business professionals, whatever their field, need to understand the structure of records and files and the potential uses of data if they are to respond quickly to both problems and opportunities. Such data generally fall into two broad categories: "How well are we doing?" data and "What's going on out there?" data. "How well are we doing?" data are concerned with internal issues like sales by territory, production costs by product type, and defect rates. Gaining access to such information and using it to reduce uncertainty in decision making are key skills. "What's going on out there?" data relate to external issues that affect the health and prosperity of the company, for example, industry trends, legal opinions, and population shifts. Private vendors like CompuServe and Dow Jones sell access to such databases.

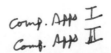

Comp. App I
Comp. App II

91

Telecommunications

Moving information off your desk (that is, from your desktop computer) to its ultimate destination will increasingly involve telecommunications—forwarding messages, reports, and financial plans electronically to another desk in the company or elsewhere in the world. But telecommunications is more than simply sending messages. Telecommunications also provides access to remote databases on the company mainframe computer, to the census data on an optical disk based in another office or building, to stock market data from Dow Jones, or to a library of reference material somewhere in your company or elsewhere. Telecommunications is the key to a world of rich, useful, and timely information that resides somewhere besides on your desk.

Statistics

Statistics are an increasingly important tool for managers. Descriptive statistics provide simple yet important information about events, places, people, or things: What proportion of the potential target population has an annual income over $35,000? What percentage of newly hired college graduates are still employed by the company after the six-month training program or after three years? Statistics also provide powerful analytical tools that help convert data into useful information. Predictive statistics tell whether the variation in things is due to more than chance. For example, a chi-square test allows us to look at how sales revenues changed at two different prices and to determine if the changes were more than just chance occurrences. We might also want to ask whether sales revenues at these two prices vary according to the region of the country. Causal analyses help us understand the specific causes and consequences of specific events: Are students from a given college more likely than those from another college to be successful in a management training program? Do college grades affect movement up the corporate ladder after ten years? Are manufacturing problems and defective products associated with the widgets supplied by Company A or with those of Company B? Are quality control problems based on night shift versus day shift effectiveness? Statistical analyses can help answer questions like these; moreover, today's desktop statistics software helps users analyze data and present the results in easy-to-read graphics.

You may wish (or need) to add other skills to your technology portfolio once you master the six basic skills. The importance of these other computer skills—programming, accounting (clearly essential if you plan to be an accountant), project management, and desktop publishing, among others—will depend on your career interests and

"SO THEN BEFORE ELECTRONIC NETWORKED BULLETIN BOARDS, HOW DID A GIRL LET A GUY KNOW SHE LIKED HIM ?"

goals. But note that our definition and description of the Technology Master do not include traditional programming skills. We see the Technology Master as someone who uses information technology resources (software, computers, raw data) to produce and access information that can then be used to make smarter, faster decisions.

Campus Profile
The University of North Texas

The University of North Texas (UNT) in Denton (just outside of Dallas) is a fairly typical metropolitan public university. It enrolls some 25,000 students, including traditional 18- to 22-year-old undergraduates from all over Texas and part-time commuters (both undergraduate- and graduate-level) from the surrounding Denton-Dallas region. The university has a good-sized undergraduate business program (some 5,600 undergraduates, with over 900 undergraduate business degrees awarded in 1988), which is accredited by the American Assembly of Collegiate Schools of Business.

What's the route to becoming a Technology Master at UNT? For future business students, the path is relatively straightforward. Dean Peter B. Lane says the College of Business Administration "is introducing computer/telecommunication technologies and the skills of learning [that are] creating the dynamics for change in business education." The College of Business Administration has its own computing center, with a large mainframe computer and sixty-four terminals, as well as a microcomputer lab with eighty-four IBM PCs. Within the college the Department of Business Computer Information Systems (BCIS), like other MIS departments in business schools, offers an array of courses "designed to provide managers with the tools and background necessary for successful careers in the rapidly changing technological environment."

UNT also has a School of Library and Information Sciences. While smaller colleges and universities do not have an entire school for information sciences, virtually every institution offers a series of basic library courses. Of specific importance to the business student is any course that offers exposure to on-line databases.

Business—Interdepartmental

Word Processing: Basic operations of word processing equipment and software. Skill development in specialized techniques and advanced applications for handling office paperwork problems through increased productivity.

Business Computer Information Systems

Introduction to Computers in Business: A study of the introductory concepts of computing in business; basic computer components, computer history, flow charting, and programming skills development. The emphasis of the course is computer technology (hardware and software), programming with an algorithmic language, and introduction to systems analysis and the use of canned programs.

Basic Information Systems: Theories, capabilities, applications, benefits, liabilities, and economics of business computer information systems. Using the computer to solve business problems. Management information systems and computer-based decision support emphasized.

Statistical Analysis I: Frequency distributions, measures of dispersion, probability, sampling estimation, and test of significance.

Statistical Analysis II: Statistical inference, nonparametric methods, variance analysis, sample design, regression and correlation, time series, and index numbers.

Library and Information Sciences

Basic Information Resources and Services: Introduction to reference methods, literature searching, and bibliographic techniques; evaluation and use of principal types of reference and other information sources; basic kinds of information services; on-line databases; reference interviews; representative problems and practice.

On-Line Information Services: Development and use of on-line information services and computerized databases in different fields; conducting on-line searches and evaluating services.

Note that the experience of UNT's business majors and nonbusiness majors who seek computer skills is *not* very different. Each type of student can tap a range of classroom, short-course, and special program options to acquire and hone technology skills. Indeed, this model is increasingly common across the country. Many campuses now require students to complete some type of computer instruction during their undergraduate years; the majority of the nation's four-year institutions offer various options for students to learn computer skills outside of formal classroom activities. Many UNT faculty members, like their colleagues at campuses across the country, use technology resources as part of the curriculum, introducing students to applications, software, and professional practice as part of their courses.

UNT faculty report that their institution has made a unique commitment to technology, at least unique among many regional state universities. It may be that UNT is unique, but it is also true that more and more campuses—public and private, universities and four-year colleges, plus a substantial proportion of community colleges—have made major investments in computing and technology. These institutions recognize their responsibility to help students acquire and develop essential technological skills.

Next Step: Taking Inventory of Your Computer Skills

So where do you go from here? How do you transform yourself into a Technology Master? We suggest you begin by taking a personal inventory of your technological skills. Go back to our list of six basic skills. How would you evaluate your skills?

The Six Basic Skills	Current Skill Level Low High					Software Product(s)
Word processing	1	2	3	4	5	_____
Spreadsheets	1	2	3	4	5	_____
Graphics	1	2	3	4	5	_____
Database management	1	2	3	4	5	_____
Telecommunications	1	2	3	4	5	_____
Statistics	1	2	3	4	5	_____

Other Technology Skills

Programming	1	2	3	4	5	_____
Accounting	1	2	3	4	5	_____
Project management	1	2	3	4	5	_____
Desktop publishing	1	2	3	4	5	_____
Other: _____	1	2	3	4	5	_____
_____	1	2	3	4	5	_____
_____	1	2	3	4	5	_____

What technological skills will make life easier for you in the coming year? What skills will help you in your classes this term? Word processing for your class papers and projects? Spreadsheets for an economics or business class? Telecommunications for access to the library card catalog or electronic mail? Data and presentation graphics for class reports? Accounting software for that introductory class in accounting?

Where do you begin? Assess your immediate needs, and then start working to develop your skills in key areas. Be patient. Like learning to ride a bike, mastering technology can take time and involve a few bruises, in this case of your ego rather than on your knees and elbows. You may feel somewhat embarrassed asking students or professors for help, but stay with it. Set some specific skill goals and then pursue them. Why? Because the benefit of mastering the technology is a lifelong skill. Unlike chemical formulas, biological phyla, or historical dates—information you memorize to fulfill class and distribution requirements (and then often quickly forget, once the immediate need is satisfied)—technological skills endure. They are essential both to your college work and to your career goals.

Shopping Tips on Buying a Computer While in College

Upwards of one fifth of today's college students own personal computers; on some campuses, every student has one. Indeed, over the past decade, computers have become as popular as stereo systems. It all began in 1984, when Apple offered aggressive discounts to college students as part of its initial efforts to promote the Macintosh. Since then, two things have happened. First, many major computer manufacturers, from Apple to Zenith, now offer special discounts to college students and faculty. Second, as the computer market has become more competitive, the price difference between the campus and the off-campus computer stores has dropped significantly.

Change comes quickly in the computer industry: New products emerge almost every six months. Consequently, there is no way we can anticipate all the innovative chips and software that will provide new features in the computers of the 1990s. However, we can offer some basic guidelines about purchasing a computer while you're in college.

- *Think About the Future.* Buy the most powerful computer you can afford. Avoid low-end machines; don't buy last year's technology. Many of today's starter or bargain systems will not run tomorrow's more sophisticated software products. Protect your investment; buy the most powerful box you can afford.

- *Consider Workgroups.* Be compatible with the people around you. For most college students, buying a computer means choosing between a Macintosh and an IBM-compatible system. Give it some careful thought before you buy. If a Mac or IBM-compatible system is the dominant product on your campus or among people in your major, then that's the system you should buy, even if you would prefer something else.

- *Don't Forget About Price.* Buy on campus. Some 600 colleges and universities have campus resale programs. Apple, Hewlett-Packard, IBM, Toshiba, NeXT, and Zenith, among others, sell their products through campus stores or via special arrangements with campus computer departments. For most students, the on-campus price will often be the best price.

Finally, a brief word about software. *Don't steal it.* Copying software, whether commercial applications or computer games, is illegal. Many campuses have special arrangements with software companies to provide special, substantial discounts to students and faculty. Moreover, virtually all corporations have strict policies about unauthorized copying of computer software. Do the right thing: Buy software; don't copy it.

6

The Problem
Solver

Problem-Solving Skills Inventory

Define problems • Exhibit intellectual curiosity • Think
abstractly/reflectively • Distinguish between fact and opinion •
Propose and evaluate solutions • Possess an open, receptive mind •
Defend a conclusion rationally • Bring reason to bear on a problem

The past three chapters of this book involved a close look at three
people: the Great Communicator, the Team Player, and the Technology Master. While the skills required to become these people are quite
different, there is at least one common thread that unites them:
information. Whether you are producing tables and charts on a computer, reading a project report, or just listening in a meeting, the
common input is information. But information processing, simply
acquiring facts and figures, is not everything. It's how you *use* the
information that really counts, how you convert data (raw facts) into
useful information. Think for a moment about the *Exxon Valdez,* the
oil tanker that dumped 11 million gallons into the pristine Alaskan
waters in April 1989. The *Valdez* captain had on the bridge (command
post) of the ship the most sophisticated equipment available. Data
galore. Still, all these data from a variety of specialized instruments
did not, or could not, prevent his tanker from running onto a reef and
causing an environmental disaster. Hundreds of companies, awash in
data, suffer small and large disasters because of management's inability *to use* information in its everyday decision making.

The major difficulty is that problem solving is messy. We prefer our lives to be neat and predictable. Consequently, we discover clever ways to maintain order. First, we ignore the mess; we tell ourselves that the problem simply does not exist. Second, we minimize it; if a problem does exist, we conclude that it isn't big enough or serious enough to deal with. Third, we delay it; in most circumstances we conclude that the problem does not require our immediate attention. And finally, if nothing else works and we are forced into problem solving, we are quite skilled at "satisficing." This means that we go for a sufficient, acceptable, or minimally satisfactory solution—not necessarily the best solution but the one that, at least momentarily, "unmesses" things.

But we live in a twenty-first-century world in which progress and problems are closely linked. Each step of progress really involves solving a problem. For example, let's say you are a senior manager at a plastics company. The invention of plastics solved the problem of cheap, nonbreakable containers for the food we eat and the beverages we drink. But is the convenience of nonrefundable bottles and microwaveable plates worth the mountains of permanent (that is, nonbiodegradable) trash we create each day? Is it worth the pollution of our harbors and the killing of sea life? Environmentalists, consumer groups, newspaper editors, and others are applying pressure: Do something about it. Fix it. When we didn't have plastics, we didn't have the problem of whether or not to use them, but now we do have the problem. Who is going to solve it? What innovations in chemistry, plastics research, and recycling will help us solve the problem we now experience because of the progress of plastic?

In a 1987 article in *Inc.* magazine entitled "Problems, Problems," Paul Hawken, chairman of a garden tool business, shares a revelation from a Saturday afternoon in the office: "The actual truth finally struck me: I would always have problems." Hawken goes on to condemn the many books on how to become a successful manager.

> *Much of it seems to rest on the assumption that problems are avoidable, and the world is controllable, if only you know which levers to pull. Too often, the authors attempt to instill certainty with checklists, must-dos, 10 principles, axioms galore, and other assorted blather. Don't buy it. The only worthwhile axioms are those designed to engage your thinking, not provide easy answers.*

So it should come as no surprise to the student planning a business career that successful and highly paid managers in any corporate enterprise display unique abilities to define problems, to seek creative and innovative solutions, and to implement timely and effective courses of action. They are the captains in a continuous problem-solving struggle.

One other note before we move along. There are many different words that are used to define the process that we discuss in this chapter: *thinking, decision making, reasoning, logic, critical thinking,* and *problem solving*. To the philosophy, psychology, or business professor there are important differences among these terms. First, let's define what we are *not* talking about when we use the term *problem solving*. We do not mean thinking or decision making. *Thinking* is too general since it is often used to describe almost anything that passes through the mind—idle daydreams, random thoughts, and loosely connected facts. A sales manager may know that district sales are going down and wish that it weren't so. While such activity does involve the processing of information, there is no conclusion or resolution. *Decision making,* on the other hand, denotes any means that leads to a course of action—or to the avoidance of action. Flipping a coin is a form of decision making. The sales manager, for example, could choose between acting now or waiting for the next sales report. Again, no resolution leads to no conclusion.

We are interested in a more dynamic, creative process. Reasoning, for example, consists of particular skills and processes involved in analyzing, evaluating, and constructing arguments. It is reasoning that makes connections between items of information. Logic is the study of reasoning. Strong reasoning skills may allow a sales manager to make a connection among three facts: (1) Sales have fallen, (2) half of the sales staff members are new to their jobs, and (3) it takes time for a sales representative to learn a new territory, understand a new product line, and cultivate new customers. Reasoning skills help the sales manager identify the factors contributing to falling sales. Reasoning skills then help this same sales manager develop strategies to address the problem: Offer more training for the new people, allow more time before pressuring the new people to produce, provide more supervision from senior district sales managers.

Finally, critical thinking and problem solving are even broader processes. For example, critical thinking is the mental process by which an event or phenomenon is investigated, using all available information, in order to reach a justifiable conclusion. Problem solving, in turn, is the application of the process of critical thinking to a specific problem, say, declining sales. This process includes problem definition: What were the sales like for the same time period last year? It includes the identification of hypotheses: Having too many new sales representatives has created an experience lag, or the entire industry is suffering a downturn due to foreign imports. It includes generating information: How many new sales representatives were hired in the past six months? What have been the industry trends for the past year? It includes conclusions: The downturn is caused by less expensive foreign imports and compounded by a new sales staff. It includes the enumeration of solutions: Pay higher commission rates to reduce the turnover of sales staff or reduce the price of the product to compete with the imports. And it involves choosing and implementing: Develop a new commission plan or issue a new price sheet.

Decision Making

Problem solving is untidy. It is tiring and difficult. It is also here to stay, which is why industry wants, and is willing to reward, the Problem Solver.

The Fourth "R"

You've probably heard about the traditional "three R's"—reading, 'riting, and 'rithmetic. Many educators now recognize a fourth R—*reasoning*. In fact, some educators and cognitive researchers identify reasoning as the most fundamental skill. Critical-thinking skills are essential for effective reading, computing, and writing.

This new emphasis on reasoning skills has led to a rush of studies and reports, many focused on elementary and high school students. For example, a 1988 report issued by the U.S. Department of Education sadly concluded that "American students read with surface understanding but have great difficulty when asked to think more deeply or to elaborate on what they have read." The study confirmed other findings that many students do not learn to analyze what they read or use information to reason effectively.

In college, problem-solving skills are often first assessed by the Scholastic Aptitude Test (SAT), widely known to many high school and college students as an admissions requirement for college. One section of the SAT deals exclusively with verbal analogies. These are verbal relationships based upon the logical analysis of the meaning of words. As a college student, you probably remember this portion of the test.

Directions: Choose the lettered pair that best expresses a relationship like that of the first pair.

1. CHICKEN : COOP
   (A) You : school
   (B) You : cage
   (C) You : car
   (D) You : farm
   (E) You : home

The reasoning follows a three-step process:

Step 1. You express the partial analogy in a very *specific* sentence, e.g., *A chicken lives in a coop.*

Step 2. You think of a word that would complete the analogy in a way that makes sense to you. For example, *A chicken lives in a coop just as you live in a house, or home, or dorm, or apartment. A chicken is a live thing, and you are a live thing. It lives in a coop, and you have to live somewhere, too.*

Step 3: You consider the answer choices and think of the very specific sentence that you made in Step 1. The completed analogy *must* fit your sentence.
 (A) *School* is okay, but you don't live there. Eliminate.
 (B) You do not live in a *cage.* Eliminate.
 (C) You do not live in a *car* either. Eliminate.
 (D) You might live *on* a farm, but not *in* one. While this may sound picky, analogies are very precise; therefore, eliminate this choice.
 (E) *Yes.* A chicken lives inside a coop, and you live inside a house. This choice best expresses the relationship.

Source: Joan Davenport Carris with William R. McQuade and Michael R. Crystal, *SAT Success* (Princeton, NJ: Peterson's Guides, 1987), p. 17.

The process of establishing a clear and necessary relationship between pairs of words—*this* follows from *that*—is also an exercise in reasoning covered in the SAT exam.

SORROW : HAPPINESS Sorrow is the opposite of happiness.
CHEMIST : LABORATORY A chemist works in a laboratory.
BED : RIVER A bed is the bottom of a river.

Teaching these skills is a tricky issue. Perhaps the trickiest part is best expressed by Richard Miller, an East Carolina University researcher: "Reasoning skill weaknesses are resistant to change. An individual student's weaknesses can be uncovered early, and yet progress can be very slow. This might be due to the fact that an 18-year-old may have been practicing incorrect patterns of reasoning for years before anyone discovers it and attempts to change it. By then the force of habit and emotional resistance powerfully interfere with attempts to reprogram his or her thought pattern." Other researchers have noted such specific weaknesses as the fact that many students equate arguments with opinions. These students analyze and evaluate arguments by merely summarizing opinions and preferences for particular ideas.

Also, although most college students know that claims or generalizations must be accompanied by supporting facts, many students do not know what counts as appropriate support or how to use supporting information and documentation effectively. For example, students tend to use anecdotes, rumors, and opinions and are often unclear about what constitutes good evidence (e.g., data, examples, principles, statements by authorities). Underdeveloped arguments are a problem. Many students provide relatively few reasons to support their claims and give little or no consideration to counterarguments or conflicting evidence. Their arguments are one-dimensional, unbalanced, and superficial.

A growing number of colleges now offer a basic skills course in critical thinking as part of a freshman core or general education program. For example, in 1981 the California State University System, which includes nineteen campuses across the state, adopted a series of General Education–Breadth Requirements that prominently featured critical-thinking skills. The university system's policy document on this change stated that "Instruction in critical thinking is to be designed to achieve an understanding of the relationship of language to logic, which should lead to the ability to analyze, criticize, and advocate ideas, to reason inductively and deductively, and to reach factual or judgmental conclusions based on sound inferences drawn from unambiguous statements of knowledge or belief." At California State University, San Bernardino, this requirement is met by allowing students to choose a freshman critical-thinking course from any one of the following areas.

Communication

Critical Thinking Through Argumentation: Principles of oral argumentation and forensics: evidence, methods of logical analysis, reasoned discourse demonstrated through argumentative speeches and debates.

Mathematics

Critical Thinking Through Problem Solving: Logical deduction. Inductive reasoning and logical deduction techniques such as analogy and generalization. Choice of appropriate representation, adequacy of given information, and strategic decisions within the problem-solving process.

❖

Who Knows?

The "Who Knows?" lesson, shown below, is one that is used in some college classes as part of critical thinking skills development in history. In this case, a primary skill involved in good problem solving is the ability to establish rules of evidence or the reliability/unreliability of sources of information.

Directions: There has been a serious plane crash in which a light plane clipped the right wing of a jumbo jet. A Government Commission has been set up to investigate the accident. As a clerk for the committee, it is your job to sift through the list of those who wish to appear before the committee to give evidence, and decide which ones should be called to give reliable data to the Commission.

The following is a list of witnesses and the location of the witnesses at the time of the accident. You should circle the names of those sources whom you believe could supply the most reliable data. Beside each name on the list, give reasons why you chose or did not choose that person.

List of Sources

1. Captain of the jet's flight crew.
2. Pilot of the small plane (bailed out prior to impact).
3. Steward on jet (was in the galley preparing food during impact).
4. Passenger No. 1 (was sitting on the left front side of the jet).
5. Passenger No. 2 (was sitting over the left wing).
6. Air Traffic Controller.
7. Airline Official in the terminal.
8. Manufacturer of light plane.
9. Representative of the aircraft insurance company.
10. Widow of man who was killed in the crash.
11. F.C.C. official who inspected both aircrafts after the crash.
12. Pathologist who performed autopsy on dead passenger.
13. Farmer who was ploughing his field below the site of the crash.
14. Steward (was in the cockpit at the time of the crash).
15. Film crew from a local TV crew who shot film of the crash from their helicopter.

Source: "Critical Thinking, the Curriculum, and the Problem of Transfer," in *Thinking: The Second International Conference,* David Perkins (editor), 1987, p. 276.

Philosophy

Critical Thinking Through Argumentation Analysis: Analysis of various kinds of reasoning employed in everyday life and in more specialized contexts, to develop each student's skill in understanding and using carefully constructed arguments.

Psychology

Critical Thinking Through Problems Analysis: Development of basic skills in critical thinking including identifying and understanding common fallacies, recognizing techniques of persuasion and propaganda, problem-solving strategies, and applying critical-thinking skills to the complex problems of everyday life.

The intent at Cal State, San Bernardino, is to provide students with a set of skills that they can apply to other classes over the course of their college careers. A few schools have been more ambitious. They have instituted programs in which critical-thinking components are built into courses within a student's major, not taught in just a single freshman core course.

The process of getting the facts is crucial to critical thinking. (See Who Knows? on page 105.) It is something that is absolutely required of a thorough accident investigator, a thoughtful historian, or a successful businessperson.

The Business Approach

In business schools, efforts to teach critical thinking or problem solving are generally accomplished in two ways: in specific problem-solving courses and more generally in "across the curriculum" approaches. One of the specific courses that can help develop the Problem Solver is in the area of statistical decision theory. (This course is often found in the mathematics department of smaller colleges.) A statistical decision theory course focuses on the use of systematic quantitative analysis to aid in the formation and making of management decisions. The name of the course and what is included in it vary greatly from one campus to another. For example, we know of three different colleges where the same material is covered in classes titled Introduction to Problem Solving, Quantitative Decision Models in Business, and Statistical Decision Theory. (This is a course that a student would take after Introduction to Statistics, perhaps in the junior year.)

A business communications course can help you develop your verbal, as opposed to quantitative, problem-solving skills. In one of our earlier testimonials (Chapter 3), Tony Branch, a vice president at Golden Gate University, stated: "I personally think that if you can't write well, particularly when you have difficulties constructing paragraphs that flow together and reach a clear, concise conclusion, this suggests that the overall conceptual thinking is muddled and not worth much. There is a real relationship. It's not just a skill which would be nice to have. Good writing is reflective of sound thinking and problem-solving abilities." In fact, one could go so far as to say that the acquisition of writing skills is the acquisition of critical-thinking skills. The examples are numerous. The ability to compose a precise topic sentence requires the global processes of defining a problem and synthesizing information. Sentences that are vague and general indicate an inability to differentiate between concrete and abstract ideas. Using conjunctive adverbs, such as *consequently, furthermore,* and *moreover,* reflects an ability to recognize cause-and-effect relationships. The ability to classify ideas and arrange them in a prescribed order—from most important to least important, general to specific, abstract to concrete—requires strong organizational and reasoning skills.

Perhaps the most common problem-solving tool in business is the case method. A businessperson is a decision maker, and, in order to make effective decisions, he or she should be able to recognize facts, reason out their connection with existing objectives and conditions, and set out a plan of action. Such skills are acquired through learning and experience and not through a favorable combination of genes. Problem solvers are made, not born.

What is the case method? A case is a real-life situation. It actually happened. It has been researched, structured, and written in such a way as to include the important facts about the company, the environment, and the people involved. The reader uses all this information to visualize the situation and to participate in the simulation of the original experience. Students, putting themselves in someone else's shoes, get a chance to rehearse judgment as they work to answer the question, "What additional information do I need? What decisions must I make? What will be the consequences of my decisions?"

For example, a case may involve the difficulties faced by a company that manufactures a very seasonal product—say, 90 percent of sales come during the Christmas season. Or perhaps a small savings and loan institution is faced with the problem of a major bank's opening a branch across the street. Or it might even be the situation that faced International Harvester in restructuring its management when it declared bankruptcy some years ago. A college professor who requires students to analyze management case studies will usually have them do the following: (1) Summarize the important material in the case, (2) identify the main problem(s), (3) develop alternative solutions to the problem, and (4) select the best alternative, based on established criteria.

The main advantage of business cases, therefore, is realism. But realism goes beyond the mere description of the situation itself because it also extends to situational problem solving. Cases help students sharpen their analytical ability in *problem finding*—filtering facts from fiction and separating the relevant from the irrelevant. Students learn to synthesize information; they also discover the process of developing and comparing different solutions. Professor Neil Paget argues in a recent *Journal of Education for Business* article entitled "Using Case Methods Effectively" that the case method is an important teaching tool in management education.

> *The case method, then, has considerable value for management education. Analytical skills are developed in a practical manner by requiring students to deal with a wide variety of realistic administrative problems. It leads to maturity and intellectual growth as students broaden their frame of reference through gradual mastery of highly complex problems in a rational manner. By requiring a high degree of mental activities on the part of the students, it leads to a heightened awareness of their own abilities and limitations and the role of others in the administrative context. Finally, the case method can develop an orientation toward action.*

Another learning technique that is becoming increasingly common in business schools is the use of a computer simulation game. For example, in April 1981 People Express was launched—and a business phenomenon took off. By the beginning of 1986 People Express had grown to be the fifth-largest airline in the United States and had revenues of about $1 billion per year. Its innovative management style and structure were praised as the wave of the future. Yet by September 1986 People Express was nearly bankrupt and was acquired at the last minute by Texas Air. What happened? The People Express Management Flight Simulator, developed by Professor John Sterman of MIT, gives the student an opportunity to find out by "flying" the company. Used as part of a human resources management or organizational behavior course, the simulator functions just as an aircraft simulator does. Sterman explains:

The students take command of the company and pilot it from startup to success. Each simulated time period they make strategic and operational decisions, and receive feedback from past decisions. The students decide how fast to grow, how to set prices, how aggressively to advertise. Hiring policies will influence morale, productivity, and turnover; marketing efforts will shape the growth of demand; competitors will fight back. They may face financial crisis or unexpected opportunity. They may go bankrupt or grow to dominate the industry. But there is no winning or losing. The purpose of the simulator is to give students insight into the issues raised by the case; to illustrate the difficulties of coordinating operations and strategy in a growth market; and to understand dynamic interconnections among a firm, its market, and its competitors.

The idea behind simulation, whether of People Express or one of the many other companies, is to allow students to launch experiments, test different problem-solving strategies, even fail— -without suffering the consequences that would take place in the real world.

Philosophy

The study of philosophy is inherently interdisciplinary; that is, many of the important areas of study in philosophy have relevance to issues in English, law, medicine, science, art, religion, and business. An area of particular relevance is the study of reasoning. This area of philosophy has evolved into two separate subdisciplines: formal and informal logic. Formal logic is mathematical in nature, and such courses (often called Symbolic Logic) are usually taken only by philosophy majors or students interested in computer systems, artificial intelligence, or other aspects of statistical reasoning.

Informal logic involves the ability to evaluate and interpret arguments and evidence of a *verbal* nature—using everyday language. Certainly the ability to evaluate good evidence versus bad evidence would be a useful managerial skill. Two financial analysts, for example, may present different conclusions to a commercial lending officer in a bank. Their presentations affect the loan officer's decision to approve a $5 million loan. How can two competent analysts come up with very different assessments about the risk involved in approving this loan request? The ability to evaluate the two different arguments and the accompanying supporting evidence is crucial.

In addition, there are several aspects of informal logic that are important to a business student besides developing stronger problem-solving skills. First, not only does a logic course involve the evaluation of arguments, but it also involves the construction of arguments.

What exactly do people in advertising do? They construct arguments that detail the benefits of a product or service in such a way that it is appealing to consumers. Second, the study of argumentation in philosophy usually contains a strong element of moral reasoning (in fact, in some smaller colleges the philosophy department is combined with a religion department). Problem solving within an ethical context has become an issue of increasing concern to industry and to society as a whole. Exxon, faced with an immense cleanup effort after the captain of the *Valdez* made his critical navigational mistake, was faced with a long series of moral choices. Viewed from one perspective, every dollar spent cleaning up the beaches of Alaska was one dollar less profit for its shareholders, most of whom have never been to Alaska.

At colleges and universities, informal or verbal logic courses have a wide variety of titles, for example, Logic, Thinking Straight, Principles of Reasoning, and Introduction to Logic and Critical Thinking.

Communications
As we have seen, many communications courses have direct application to the industry skills that you should acquire: the Great Communicator and public speaking, the Team Player and interpersonal communications, etc. Many communication departments also offer a course in argumentation and debate that involves reasoning, strategy, and oral advocacy. This course would be useful to the aspiring advertising executive who is making a presentation or pitch to a new account. It would also be helpful to a future corporate public relations officer who is continually faced with the challenge of turning problems into opportunities. In both of these situations and many others in business, the requisite skill involves the development and analysis of arguments in all kinds of public presentations, speeches, interviews, and meetings.

Computer Science
We have already had a thorough discussion about computers in Chapter 5. In this chapter we look to the computer science department on campus not for the technical skills needed to move data but for the process skills associated with good problem solvers. Most introductory programming courses focus on a small number of widely used programming languages—COBOL, BASIC, FORTRAN, and Pascal. But perhaps most important, these courses help you learn to structure your thinking. Remember, the computer is stupid; it will do only what you tell it to do. So your thought processes, the steps you want the machine to take, must be crisp and clear and offer no possibility of misinterpretation.

Kathy Wohlford's successes in the banking industry defy some of the numbers. While almost three out of four persons in banking today are women, only a small percentage of them have risen to senior management level. Kathy, however, is already a vice president and group products manager at California's Glendale Federal Bank. She came to Glendale after six years with the Bank of America, where she began as a management trainee straight out of Cal State Fullerton's business program. Nine months after starting with B of A, Kathy was an operations officer at a local branch, reporting to the branch manager. She then moved on to manage the customer service unit for all of B of A's southern California automatic teller machine (ATM) network—*all 635 machines.*

"My position was a bit scary. If you made a mistake, it could cost the company a great deal of aggravation and serious customer relations problems. I had to refine my problem-solving skills in such a way that all options would be explored and analyzed before I made a decision. One of the tools I began using religiously was a flow chart. I was first exposed to 'charting' in a computer programming course at Fullerton. It allows you to show the sequence of events that comprise a process. It makes you think in terms of logical steps."

Kathy is now responsible for Glendale Federal's ATM network, as well as managing the retail delivery of checking and savings accounts. "You know, I began doing flow charts and cause-and-effect diagrams in my programming and management case classes in college. Almost ten years later, I am still learning how important it is to be able to logically work through problems. In my industry, the career path is littered with people who seemingly have all the skills necessary to be successful. But all it takes is one critical mistake on a major decision and everyone begins questioning your judgment—'Is she in over her head? Can she handle this level of responsibility?' My decision-making skills, my ability to develop and evaluate arguments and to enumerate options, have had a lot to do with my still being a 'survivor' on the path."

Campus Profile
Edmonds Community College

Edmonds Community College is located just to the north of Seattle in Washington State's Puget Sound region. As a public, two-year, state-funded community college, Edmonds provides a wide variety of instructional programs that lead to an associate degree (with options to transfer to a four-year college) or to a vocational certificate. First, Edmonds' college transfer programs are designed to fulfill general education requirements for students planning to transfer to four-year colleges and universities. The result is an Associate of Arts or Associate of Sciences degree in such fields as biology, economics, math, or sociology. Second, occupational education programs at the college are designed to prepare students for specific jobs or to improve existing job skills. An Associate of Technical Arts degree is earned by completing the requirements in one of these programs—for example, accounting, allied health, electronics, or small-business management.

Several years ago, Edmonds, like many other community colleges nationwide, began to take a closer look at its general education program, the series of required courses that all students must take. A task force on General Education, chaired by Mary Hale, a business instructor, came to an important realization: "Even though we were a community college, we were beginning to see too much of a stress on task-oriented skills. We decided to implement a system that would ensure a broader base of life skills." The skill areas that Edmonds began to emphasize were these:

Communication: Written and oral skills required. May also include electronic communications and/or keyboarding/word processing skills.

Human relations: May include leadership, appropriate interpersonal, intercultural life, stress management, and/or adapting-to-change skills. Course work in humanities and psychology may be appropriate in some instances.

Problem solving: May include computational, reasoning, computer, and/or programming skills.

Each department set out to meet these new skill requirements, either through reorienting current courses to include communications, human relations, and problem-solving sections or by developing new courses. For example, students pursuing an Associate of Technical Arts degree in accounting are required to take a three-course accounting sequence that includes a laboratory component involving computer simulation exercises.

In addition to a general education emphasis, students at Edmonds can bolster their problem-solving skills by enrolling in the following courses.

Introduction to Logic: Basic principles of inductive and deductive logics; practical methods of evaluating arguments.

Analytical Thinking: Using materials from varied humanities disciplines, this course gives students rigorous practice in the cognitive skills common to the humanities: perception, ordering, classification, memory, use of abstract and figurative language, and selection of appropriate problem-solving strategies.

Introduction to Computer Programming: A beginning class in computer programming using the BASIC computer language. The class is designed to acquaint students with general problem-solving skills and the techniques of computer programming used to deal with these problems. Students learn to logically analyze a problem and to write, correct, and test computer solutions.

Ivory Tower Information

Why don't colleges spend more time teaching students the kind of critical-thinking skills needed to be successful in business—and in life? One reason is that most professors, regardless of field, do not distinguish between problem solving as an acquired skill and problem-solving skills as one of the outcomes of their courses. While there is thinking going on in all these instances, it is very different from a generalizable notion of critical thinking and problem solving that is a deliberate skill.

Another reason is that problem solving is often seen to be no more than intelligence in action. According to Edward de Bono, a noted researcher and author in this area, "Two conclusions can be drawn from this: for people with high intelligence, nothing need be done about their thinking; for people with more humble intelligence, nothing can be done." De Bono uses an automobile analogy to illustrate: "Innate intelligence is the engineering and the horsepower of the car. Critical thinking is the skill with which the car is driven. A high-powered car may be driven badly, and a more humble car may be driven well." The common assumption that students who do well on examinations are good problem solvers is, therefore, not necessarily correct.

A final reason is a misunderstanding about information. For the most part, the type of thinking involved in most college courses is based upon an "ivory tower" assumption: the availability of information. A multiple-choice examination asks a question and then provides five answers. The assumption is that if you've taken good lecture notes and read the text, you will be able to choose the correct answer. You have all the information necessary to solve the problem. But that kind of thinking is not what happens "out there." A manager rarely has more than 25 to 30 percent of the information needed to make a decision. It would be like taking a final examination, based on a textbook that had two thirds to three quarters of its chapters removed before you had a chance to study them.

Not only is the information not available, but the quality of the information that is available is often highly questionable. When you take a college midterm or final, you know you can rely on two experts, the professor and the author of the textbook, both of whom are fully informed. They give you truths—or at least the answers you need to do well on the test! Real life (and real business), alas, are very different. In business you rely on all sorts of highly imperfect information: a three-year-old survey of consumers, the late-night stories of a sales rep, two junior analysts who are competing for a promotion, and a colleague who has always been envious of your success. Some of the information you receive is accurate and factual, some is inaccurate and impressionistic, and some may simply be wrong and out of date. Your responsibility is to sift through the facts, partial facts, fiction, and self-serving arguments to make a decision.

The Problem Solver, the individual pursued by industry, does not confuse opinions with arguments or association with causality. He or she can both evaluate arguments and construct them. Or as Professor Raymond Corey of Harvard Business School observes, "The ability to think incisively, to use evidence judiciously, to recognize hidden assumptions, and to follow to the end the often tortuous implications of a line of reasoning is an essential skill of management."

The problem-solving skills discussed in this chapter can never be acquired through a business class true-false, multiple-choice, or fill-in-the-blanks examination. The skills described by Raymond Corey are developed and enhanced from courses in logic, argumentation and debate, and quantitative decision models. These classes exist at every college. These skills are nurtured by doing case studies, searching for additional information, and asking questions. They are there for the asking. They are there for the taking.

7

The Foreign Ambassador

Multicultural Skills Inventory

Get along with other people • Be tolerant of foreign cultures • Be able to speak foreign languages • Maintain openness to different ideas • Develop a global, not an ethnocentric, perspective • Be aware of cultural differences • Be able to adjust to new conditions • Have no fixed prejudices • Be curious about new situations • Understand the interdependence of nations in a global economy

In the late 1960s Jean-Jacques Servan-Schreiber, a noted European economist, writer, and founder of the influential French newspaper *L'Exprès* (akin in influence to the *New York Times* or the *Washington Post* in the United States), began writing about the economic challenges confronting the United States and the world. His influential 1968 book, *The American Challenge*, predicted that American investment in Europe—that is, American companies that set up European divisions—would be the next rising economic world power. These American companies based in Europe seemed likely to overshadow European-based companies owned and operated by French, German, British, Italian, Irish, Spanish, and other European nationals. Servan-Schreiber's analysis was done in the shadow of the increasingly visible U.S. influence on the European and world economy: U.S. companies, aided by a strong dollar and the competitive health of U.S. manufacturing technologies, were investing heavily in Europe and Asia. U.S. investment abroad and particularly in Europe, according to Servan-Schreiber, would emerge as a leading economic force in the world.

How the world has changed in two decades! Today, it is foreign investment in the United States that has emerged as the world's newest and most potent economic power. The facts are hard to ignore. Assisted by the falling value of the dollar, Japanese investment in the United States doubled between 1983 and 1987; it has continued to double annually for the past several years. Japanese, European, and other foreign corporations now own some very "American" companies:

- The French technology conglomerate Groupe Bull now owns both Honeywell Inc. (a large mainframe computer vendor) and Zenith Data Systems (a major U.S. manufacturer of desktop and laptop computers).

- Sony, the Japanese electronics giant, acquired CBS Records in 1988 for the modest price of $2 billion. Sony subsequently purchased Columbia Pictures for $3.4 billion in 1989.

- Aoki Corporation purchased the Westin Hotels and Resorts chain, formerly owned by the parent company of United Air Lines Inc., in 1988.

- Bertelsmann AG, a German conglomerate, now counts RCA Records, Doubleday Books, and *Parents* magazine in its portfolio.

- Japanese interests bought the headquarters buildings of Exxon and Mobil, as well as Rockefeller Center, in New York City and Arco Plaza in Los Angeles.

- Toyota, Nissan, and Honda all built car manufacturing plants in the Midwest and maintain automotive design centers in California. Honda now *exports* Ohio-made Accords to Japan.

- Heileman G. Brewing Company Inc., a Midwestern company that is one of the largest brewers in the United States, became a subsidiary of the Bond Corporation, an Australian conglomerate, in 1986.

"CBS Evening News" reports that foreigners now hold over one trillion five hundred billion U.S. dollars and assets. In 1988 alone there were 307 foreign acquisitions of U.S. companies, everything from farmland, fast food, hotels, office buildings, and communications companies to steel and oil. Yet, even with the rising tide of foreign investment in the United States, Americans have still been busy investing abroad. (See Table 8 showing the nations, including the United States, with the most foreign investments in other countries worldwide.) The largest Kentucky Fried Chicken restaurant is in China. Japan's second-leading breakfast cereal is Gennmai Flakes, a

Table 8. Direct Foreign Investment in Other Countries, Worldwide

(in millions of U.S. dollars)

	1960	1970	1980	1986
United States	$2,940	$7,589	$19,220	$28,050
Japan	79	355	2,385	14,480
West Germany	139	876	4,180	8,999
Britain	700	1,308	11,360	16,691
Canada	52	302	2,694	3,254

Source: Ricard Kirkland, "Entering a New Age of Boundless Competition," *Fortune,* March 14, 1988, p. 40.

Kellogg's export in which ground whole rice is substituted for corn. Russians are taking classes at Hamburger U, the internationally known corporate training center run by McDonald's: the first graduates now run the world's largest McDonald's—in Moscow! General Mills has made inroads in Asia with Cheerios—pronounced "Cherry Ohs" by the Japanese. T. Boone Pickens, the prominent U.S. corporate takeover artist, recently acquired 32 million shares of Koito Manufacturing, a maker of halogen lights and other auto parts for Toyota. The *Wall Street Journal* launched a daily Asian edition of the newspaper in 1989. *Fortune* recently launched a French version of its magazine; *Better Homes and Gardens* now exists in Australia and Korea.

And the European action is just beginning. U.S. and European companies are engaged in frantic planning and posturing for 1992, the year when the traditional economic, monetary, and political boundaries fall in the twelve European Common Market nations, creating the largest corporate and consumer market in the world. U.S. firms are working feverishly to establish a Continental presence before 1992 (or to enhance their existing operations). One company has already begun. In the muddy sugar-beet fields 20 miles west of Paris, bulldozers are tracing the outlines of some familiar sights: Main Street, Pirates of the Caribbean, and the Mad Tea Party teacup ride. Yes, in 1992 the Walt Disney Company will open a $2.6 billion extravaganza—Euro Disneyland.

Moreover, the political upheaval that brought down the Iron Curtain in 1989 and 1990 has created another wave of business opportunities—eagerly pursued by American, European, and Asian companies—in Eastern Europe.

This dizzying array of international moves is a natural extension of a shrinking planet. Fax machines send contracts, letters, and diagrams across continents and oceans in a matter of minutes. Satellite-linked electronic networks speed ever greater volumes of information around the world at ever lower costs. Some 350 million travelers a year now venture outside their own borders, compared with just 25 million in 1950. The term *global community,* almost a science-fiction notion a few years ago, is fast becoming a reality. Our increasing interdependence is accompanied by the emergence of a truly *global economy.* The result is that more and more businesses are developing global game plans, a series of strategies that know few geographic boundaries. As John F. Welch Jr., CEO of General Electric, has noted, "Globalization is no longer an objective but an imperative, as markets and geographic barriers become increasingly blurred and even irrelevant."

Heinz, for example, has a geographic strategy to make "theirs a company of worldwide brands," according to Walter Schmid, vice president of corporate planning. In 1987 Heinz purchased Spain's leading purveyor of *tomates fritos* (fried tomatoes), a product found in almost every Spanish home, used for all kinds of sauces and recipes. Schmid notes, "In each part of the globe, we seek to establish a leading market presence anchored by respected and popular brands." Coca-Cola has a similar global perspective, detailed in How Coke Markets to the World. (See page 119.)

In 1989 global soft drink operations contributed income equal to the total generated by the entire company just four years earlier. In fact, Coca-Cola earned more money from soft drinks in Japan than it did in the United States. Similarly, Coke's nemesis in the United States, Pepsi, has its own global strategy. In the largest deal ever between a U.S. corporation and the Soviet Union, Pepsico Inc. signed an agreement in 1990 to barter Pepsi-Cola for vodka. The $3 billion deal will see Pepsi take its profits not in cash, but in Stolichnaya vodka, which it will sell in this country.

What does all this have to do with you, the student at Jersey City State College, Cal State Chico, Notre Dame, or Whittier College? Are these developments too remote to affect you? Quite the contrary. There is a good chance that this growing global interdependence will have a direct impact on your career in business. You may not think of yourself as a globe-trotting executive for Coca-Cola, Heinz, or General Mills, but there is a significant likelihood that you could begin working for a U.S. multinational firm; by the year 2000 almost one out of

How Coke Markets to the World

What brands of soda do you think would be available if you walked into a grocery store in Singapore? Or in Copenhagen? Or in Buenos Aires? Chances are good that one of your choices would be Coke. The Coca-Cola Company, based in Atlanta, Ga. (where Coke was invented 102 years ago), now operates in 155 countries worldwide. To penetrate these markets, Coca-Cola had to overcome many country-specific problems. It also had to find the most effective way to sell its products throughout the world. The solution, according to Ira C. Herbert, Coke's chief marketing officer, was *global marketing;* that is, think globally, but act locally.

What are some of the cultural considerations in marketing that a multinational like Coca-Cola must be aware of? "We have to know how Coca-Cola is used with food. In Argentina, for example, a high percentage of our product is consumed with food; in other countries, it is not. In such locations, Coca-Cola is strictly a refreshment beverage that is used on its own. Obviously, the thrust of our business is to increase the times that Coca-Cola is consumed during the day and to expand the age group that our products appeal to. Our marketing efforts attempt to ensure that a soft drink, specifically Coca-Cola, becomes a part of their lives."

Are the company's products ever tailored to a specific audience? "We have a number of products that are tailored to a specific country or to a specific geography. For example, in Brazil, we make a product called Guarana Tai. In northern Latin America we make another product called Fanta-Kolita, which is a cream soda type of drink."

Coca-Cola is attempting to expand its reach into the huge Asian marketplace. How do you view this market, and how does the company intend to increase consumption in China, Thailand, and Indonesia? "We view the Asian market as having unlimited potential. It's an enormous opportunity for us, and we are working very hard to develop these markets. We now have seven bottling plants in China and other facilities under construction. We're working very diligently in that country to extend our distribution. We already have a significant foothold in Indonesia. In other parts of Asia, we are working to build a basic infrastructure of distribution and brand-building, which will allow us to realize the potential that can be tapped by marketing to this enormous number of people."

Source: Abstracted from "How Coke Markets to the World: An Interview with Ira C. Herbert." Reprinted with permission from *Journal of Business Strategy*, September/October 1988, Vol. 9, No. 5. Copyright © by Warren, Gorham & Lamont, Inc., 210 South Street, Boston, MA 02111.

every three U.S. companies will be conducting business abroad. And at the rate that the British, Canadians, and Japanese are "buying American," there is even a good chance that you may be working for a foreign-based company. You, as a Foreign Ambassador? It may happen.

SNAPSHOTS

CYPLEX was founded in 1981 by Dick Morley and Larry Hill. Dick Morley has been involved in the start-up of over twenty high-tech companies, including Andover Controls and Modicon. Larry Hill was a Modicon employee, and together they decided to develop products for industrial communications, as CYPLEX. The company's primary market has been in automated material-handling systems, which enable noncontact communication with crane and monorail systems, as well as communication between moving vehicles and a guidance wire buried in a factory floor. The company currently employs ten people in Hollis, New Hampshire, and makes extensive use of engineering contractors in specialty areas.

Although a small firm, the company currently exports approximately 20 percent of its products. This global perspective has been provided by Matt Pierson, a 1983 marketing graduate from the University of Rhode Island. In college Matt participated in the Semester at Sea program sponsored by the University of Pittsburgh. The program involves sailing around the world for 100 days—50 spent at sea and 50 spent traveling in twelve countries. All courses taught at sea have an international emphasis. According to Matt, "Those three months were an awakening for me. Everywhere I went there were different customs, new ways of interacting with people. It was a tremendous learning experience, being in situations in which none of your own norms applied. You were literally on 'foreign ground' and had to reorient your thinking and actions to reflect your current environment. As a marketing student, I also saw the opportunities, the value of looking to markets beyond the borders of your state or country."

And Matt Pierson, the seagoing college student, has become his company's Foreign Ambassador. In 1988 he represented the state of New Hampshire on a high-tech trade mission to the People's Republic of China. CYPLEX has opened up new markets in Sweden and West Germany and, under Matt's leadership, expects its export share of revenues to climb to over 50 percent by 1992. Not bad for a college kid from Rhode Island.

Any way that you look at it, a college graduate who has a limited view of the world is at a disadvantage. Multicultural skills may not merely be nice to have in this new global economy; they may be the very reason that you get a job. For the Jersey City, Chico, Notre Dame, or Whittier student, therefore, the time to begin gaining these skills is *now*.

Preparing for Global Citizenship

People who think that their cultural values, beliefs, or religion is superior to all others possess ethnocentric attitudes. Unfortunately, ethnocentricity usually surfaces in the form of patronization, superiority, disrespect, indifference, or inflexibility. One form of ethnocentricity is stereotyping, the tendency to view things in a universal form without individuality. Business Professor Rose Knotts at the University of North Texas, in Denton, relates the following story:

> A man attending an international relations banquet was seated across from another man who possessed Asian physical characteristics. Wishing to advance international relations, he asked the Asian, "Likee foodee?" The man politely nodded his head. During the program, the Asian was introduced as an award-winning professor of economics at a prestigious university and was asked to make a few projections about world trade imbalances. After a brief discussion in perfect English, the Asian professor sat down, glanced across at his astonished neighbor and asked, "Likee talkee?"

While the story may warrant a chuckle, the sad fact is that Americans and U.S. corporations are poorly prepared to live and compete in a global community. Indeed, many U.S. companies have had results ranging from mild embarrassment to outright disaster. Seemingly harmless brand names, logos, and advertising phrases can take on unintended or hidden meaning when ignorantly translated into other languages or imported into cultures. Examples are numerous. One of the first errors came in the 1920s when Coca-Cola first marketed soft drinks in China. It developed a group of Chinese characters that, when pronounced, sounded like the product name. Unfortunately, the literal translation of the characters was "Bite the wax tadpole."

More recently automobile makers have made their share of international blunders. Chevrolet's Nova translated into Spanish as *No va*—"It doesn't go." Ford introduced its Fiera truck to a number of Spanish-speaking countries only to learn that the name means "ugly old woman" in Spanish. And General Motors' "Body by Fisher" slogan became "Corpse by Fisher" when translated into Japanese. Even more modest products cannot escape the problem of translation. Sunbeam entered the German market with its Mist-Stick hair-curling iron; as might be expected, Sunbeam found that German women had little use or desire for a product marketed as a "manure wand." Paramount's early Japanese translations of the movie title "Black Rain" made no sense to native Japanese speakers; they reported that "black" was correctly translated, but "rain" looked like a meaningless string of characters instead of a real word.

Business professionals operating in an international marketplace must also be acutely aware of each country's culture and traditions. A culture teaches a subtle set of attitudes and beliefs that result in distinctive standards, mores, and lifestyles in virtually every country. It is also interesting to recall a few of the cultural errors that U.S. companies have made in overseas markets. In Japan, picture frames aimed at the office market sold poorly: Cultural traditions dictate that family pictures not be kept on office desks, which are viewed only as places of work. The Japanese place family photographs in albums and show them only to friends in the privacy of their homes. And in Africa, men were cool to a U.S. firm's commercial for a men's deodorant that showed a happy male being chased by beautiful women. The African interpretation was that the deodorant would make men weak and susceptible to being overrun by women.

How are our colleges and universities responding? Let's look at the current situation. In a summer 1989 article on the future of business school curricula, *Fortune* magazine reported that "the MBA of the future should speak a foreign language fluently and be intimate with a foreign culture, Japanese preferred in both cases." A 1989 report prepared by the National Governors' Association states emphatically: "Knowledge of other languages is essential for business and trade with economic competitors. Foreign language study can be an important bridge to the understanding of other cultures. . . . All college and university graduates must be knowledgeable about the broader world and conversant in another language." In spite of this, only 9 percent of U.S. colleges require a foreign language for the undergraduate degree. Is language incompetence a problem? It is, according to some people:

> *How are we to sell our products in a global economy when we neglect to learn the language of the customer? How are we to open overseas markets when other cultures are only dimly understood?*
>
> Gerald L. Baliles, governor of Virginia, 1989

> *One reason Americans find it so difficult to do business with the rest of the world is that they are so ignorant of it. International comparisons of the number of Americans learning foreign languages rank the nation woefully low.*
>
> The Economist, May 16, 1987

Widespread culture innocence and language illiteracy is one of the three factors of prime importance in resolving the persistent U.S. trade deficits.

Arthur Whitehill, *Business Horizons,* January–February 1988

And the problem is not merely one of language; it extends to an understanding of foreign cultures and values and how they compare with U.S. cultures, values, and traditions. The concern for the business student needs to extend beyond whether to take French, German, Spanish, or Japanese. Indeed, Ernest Boyer, president of the Carnegie Foundation for the Advancement of Teaching, stated in his recent book *College: The Undergraduate Experience in America:* "After visiting dozens of colleges and universities with hundreds of faculty members and students, we are forced to conclude that a dangerous parochialism pervades many higher learning institutions. While some students have a global perspective, the vast majority, although vaguely concerned, are inadequately informed about the interdependent world in which they live."

Becoming adequately informed about the interdependent world requires cross-cultural training. A society's culture has tremendous influence on the lives of its members. It affects how they think, behave, and feel, and, along with a common language, it determines what is unique about them. For the business student, therefore, his or her college experiences should lead to an increased sensitivity to cultural differences. The cultural environment that we speak of includes not only language but customs, religion, status and social relationships, values and beliefs, and legal and political traditions.

Acquiring the Skills

It is apparent that a manager in the turbulent international environment must be more than a skilled professional. He or she must also possess a deep realization of cultural diversity and the capacity to adjust his or her skills and strategies accordingly. A business student attempting to acquire the skills of the Foreign Ambassador might look to five broad areas: general education, individual business courses, international business major, exchange programs, and interdisciplinary programs.

General Education

According to the Carnegie Foundation for the Advancement of Teaching, 95 percent of all four-year colleges offer general education in the form of distribution requirements. That is, a certain proportion of courses must be taken from the humanities, natural sciences, and social sciences divisions in the institution. A humanities requirement can be satisfied through courses that range from architectural history to German to philosophy; in the natural sciences, from biology and physics to chemistry; and in the social sciences, from anthropology to sociology to economics. One college catalog states that, through a general education program, students become "well-educated, thoughtful, and responsible human beings, understanding themselves and the world around them."

You may recall from the conclusion of The Great Communicator chapter the story about the freshman marketing majors who registered for junior-level business courses. The students were convinced that the only truly important courses in college were in business, their major. These were the courses that would get them a job. Such students, ones that see college as an exercise in job training, tend to view general education as something to "get out of the way," not as an opportunity to gain perspective.

Yet the foundation of the multicultural skills shown to be critical to businesspeople of the twenty-first century is developed in the social sciences, for example, in anthropology. Courses like cultural and social anthropology investigate cross-cultural religious beliefs and social interaction. At some schools—UCLA, for example—there are even specialized courses in regional cultures: Latin American Communities, Civilizations of South Asia, Cultures of the Middle East, and Japan. In sociology there are courses like Social Stratification and Comparative and Historical Sociology, studying the development of different social systems. In economics there are numerous courses that are intercultural in nature. At Swarthmore College, for example, there are The International Economy and Comparative Economic Systems.

Finally, it should also be noted that upper-division (junior- and senior-level) courses in most languages also provide extensive skill development. Beyond composition, translation, and speaking courses, language departments explore the cultures of the countries in which specific languages are spoken.

General education at a college or university is designed to impart broad, liberal learning skills that stand in contrast to the technical skills that are the major orientation of most business programs. A concentration on narrow skills, without a cultural base, can be disastrous, as we saw in our list of international blunders. Or as Will Rogers, the old-time humorist once said, "There is nothing so stupid as an educated man if you get off the thing that he was educated in."

Individual Business Courses

Business schools have responded to the need for a more globally educated graduate in two distinct ways. First, many schools have developed a broad-sweeping international business course that emphasizes the shifting cultural environments in which one-world business takes place. Eckerd College in Florida offers, for example, a course called The Cultural Environment of International Business. Aimed at undergraduates interested in international business, the course systematically relates eight categories of culture—language, religion, values and attitudes, social organization, education, technology and material culture, politics, and law—to the operations of multinational firms. Also, it summarizes features of different national cultures and describes examples of successful and unsuccessful cross-cultural adaptation on the part of business firms. Second, business schools have taken their standard courses in marketing, management, finance, and so on and added internationalized versions, resulting in a proliferation of course work. (See Table 9.) For instance, one of the more popular courses, International Finance, is geared to students who are likely to confront the international dimensions of corporate financial management, that is, extending financial decision making to the international setting, including foreign exchange markets, the international monetary system, and import and export financing.

Table 9. Curriculum Content Related to International Business

(percentage of the 750 American Assembly of Collegiate Schools of Business–member undergraduate programs that offer courses on the following subjects or issues)

Undergraduate Programs	% Offering
International Marketing course	68
International Economics course	61
International Business course	54
International Finance course (macro)	40
International Management course	33
International Financial Management course	31
International Accounting	20
Multinational Corporations course	14
International Business Law	11

Source: Duane Kajawa, "Internationalization of Management Education," in *Languages and Communication for World Business and the Professions Conference Proceedings,* May 1987, p. 9.

Another course that is now being offered on a growing number of campuses is International Business Communications. At Illinois State University, for example, the course deals with oral and written communications in foreign cultures. Specifically, students explore the differences in tone and formality of both verbal and nonverbal interactions between businesspeople from Saudi Arabia, Japan, Mexico, and France. Cross-cultural negotiating and conflict management skills are examined, as is the organization of letters and reports.

International Business Major

General education programs contain broad opportunities for multicultural skill acquisition, as do the individual courses in a business program. Some students, however, may be interested in a more coordinated, focused program in international business. Almost one in four AACSB-member business schools now offers an international business major. Beyond the basic introductory courses in business, such programs require that you take a minimum number of courses that have an international perspective. In addition, they may require fluency in a second language. (See page 127.)

Exchange Programs

One of the best ways to acquire multicultural skills is to travel abroad—to extend the campus beyond its walls and make connections with other cultures and peoples. As we have seen, while only a small proportion of undergraduate students actually study abroad, the opportunity to do so is available at most colleges and universities. In *College: The Undergraduate Experience in America,* Ernest Boyer cites the following examples.

- *The State University of New York* has had a Russian exchange program with Moscow State University for more than ten years.

- *Brown University* offers an undergraduate exchange program with countries in Eastern Europe. Arrangements with the Germans enable students from Brown to study each year for a semester or summer at Wilhelm Pieck University in Rostock on the Baltic coast.

- *The University of Virginia*'s department of Spanish, Italian, and Portuguese languages runs a spring semester program in Valencia, Spain. Students live with Spanish families as well as receive instruction in Spanish related to aspects of literature, culture, and civilization.

Business Schools Must Make Language Fluency a Top Priority

The approach of 1992, when Europe will become a unified economic giant, has focused attention in the United States on the preparedness of American business to compete in world markets. Opinions vary on subjects such as isolationism, potential trade barriers, and protectionism, but no one has any doubts about one glaring weakness in the fabric of American business: language training.

Throughout most of the second half of the 20th century, the American way of doing business has been admired and emulated. In increasing numbers, foreign students have flocked to American universities to obtain master's degrees in business administration. Business schools in colleges and universities all over the U.S. have flourished, creating programs, obtaining grants, and issuing diplomas. When one examines the "international" programs of these business schools, however, one finds a shocking absence of requirements that students attain fluency in one or more foreign languages.

Throughout the entire "educational" process in international business, faculties naively assume that the fundamentals of business do not include fluency in our competitors' tongues. European and Japanese business schools, on the other hand, demand that their students be fluent in at least one foreign language and often insist that they complete yearlong internships in a country where that language is spoken, before they can receive a degree.

Foreign-language departments in American universities have been no more sensitive to their students' needs than have business schools. One would assume that they would be interested in seeing their graduates go forth able to use their skills in many different settings. But are language majors encouraged to take courses that would give them fluency in the terminology used in foreign business procedures? No. Business and language departments should overcome their indifference to or distrust of each other and pursue the common goal of training fully rounded businesspeople. Fluency in speaking foreign languages and sophisticated understanding of foreign cultures must be seen as positive, admirable, and highly beneficial. . . .

Source: Abstracted from John C. Bednar, *The Chronicle of Higher Education*, February 7, 1990, p. B2.

- *Duke University* offers an annual program of study in the People's Republic of China, at both Nanjing University and Beijing Teachers College. Language training in Beijing is followed by a semester of study at Nanjing in literature, anthropology, and history.

And beyond these specific programs at individual colleges and universities, virtually every student can take advantage of national organizations, such as the Institute of European Studies, located in Chicago, which arrange various international education experiences for U.S. college students.

Interdisciplinary Programs

While general education, international business courses and majors, and study-abroad programs have been around for a long time, there is one new approach to becoming the Foreign Ambassador. A growing number of colleges and universities have begun to develop an interdisciplinary major in business and a foreign language. For example, a program at Mississippi State University provides students with both general education and expertise in four areas of study essential for a career in world trade: fluency in at least one foreign language, proficiency in a second foreign language, expertise in domestic and international business practices, and awareness of the history and political systems of the country of the first foreign language. As the Mississippi State course catalog says, "The new program has provided new focus for previously independent courses of study on foreign languages, business foreign languages, domestic and international business, history, and political science by blending them into a degree program."

An even more comprehensive approach is taken at Eastern Michigan University. The university recently began offering a joint-degree program that awards a Bachelor of Business Administration *and* a Bachelor of Arts in Languages and World Business. The program is a modification of two existing degree programs. The language degree is in applied German, French, Spanish, or Japanese, with specialized cultural studies, and is joined with a major in international business administration. The result is a five-year program that includes a cooperative placement in a foreign business during the spring and summer sessions of the fourth year.

Campus Profile
The University of Miami

Let's take a closer look at the curricular options available to students at the University of Miami in Florida. The University of Miami is a selective independent university of some 8,000 undergraduates. While Miami offers a wide variety of courses and majors, fully 23 percent of the baccalaureate degrees are awarded in business and management. Although just under half of the university's students come from Florida, almost 10 percent, some 700 students, are from foreign countries.

Like most other colleges and universities, the University of Miami has a general education program. The university catalog, like those of hundreds of campuses across the country, offers a reasonable rationale for the general education program and accompanying course requirements:

> *The University of Miami is dedicated to providing an opportunity for students to become more socially competent, to increase their personal intellectual development, and to acquire occupational and professional preparation. Students have different goals, but the University recognizes that all require a proper foundation from which to develop their individual paths to knowledge. The General Education Requirements reflect this philosophy, specifying broad area distribution requirements which can be fulfilled by a variety of course offerings.*

All undergraduate degree candidates, therefore, are required to take courses in the fine arts, arts and humanities, natural sciences, and social sciences.

How might the aspiring ambassador use the general education program at a place like the University of Miami to develop a better understanding of foreign cultures? Several multicultural courses satisfy general education requirements:

General Education

Principles of Cultural Anthropology: Cultural anthropology, including such topics as economics, politics, kinship, families, health systems, religion and personality.

Cultural Dynamics: A cross-cultural examination of the causal factors in changing cultural scenes.

International Economics: Study of the principles of international trade and investment and balance-of-payments adjustment, application to current problems in international economics relations.

The business school at the University of Miami has also made a commitment to developing Foreign Ambassador skills: "The School of Business Administration motivates and prepares men and women for positions of leadership in business and government, in the local, national and international communities." And to that end, the business school offers a broad range of courses that have a global orientation.

Business

International Business: An introduction to the theory and institutions relevant to the conduct of business internationally: includes an overview of current business patterns and their historical antecedents; social systems in countries as they affect the conduct of business from one country to another; basic assessment of international activities that fall within functional disciplines; and analysis of alternative ways in which international business may evolve in the future.

Other courses include: International Accounting and Taxation; International Business Law; International Financial Management; International Banking; International Insurance and Reinsurance; International Marketing; International and Multinational Management; and Comparative and International Industrial Relations.

While smaller institutions will have a few language courses, the advantage of a larger school like Miami is often in the breadth of its course work. For example:

Languages

Arabic, Chinese, French, German, Hebrew, Italian, Japanese, Portuguese, Russian, and Spanish.

And finally, the University of Miami student who wanted to specialize in international trade could major in international finance and marketing in the business school. Also, the university has an active Office of International Programs; for example, aspiring ambassadors could study the state of the art of European business practices by spending a semester at the Aston Management Centre in Birmingham, England.

Send Us Your Sons—and Daughters

In a recent article entitled "International Curriculum for the Professions," the author opens with a plea: "The changing role of the United States in the world demands that 'the average citizen,' as well as public officials, politicians and business and industrial leaders at all levels, develop a better understanding of the international world in which we all live and work together."

This plea is consistent with our awareness of the need for the Foreign Ambassador, but the pure and simple truth is that achieving a one-world mentality does not come naturally to most of us. People tend to cling to and cluster around others who are like themselves.

Every major city in the United States has its racial and ethnic enclaves: Italian, Polish, Jewish, African-American, Chicano, Chinese, Japanese. Sections of London seem to be reserved for Pakistanis and immigrants from India. Such self-imposed segregation always seems to result in misunderstandings. We don't quite understand others, their actions, their ways. And we are often irritated by the fact that they, the foreigners, don't try hard enough to behave like us, dress like us, and think like us. (See below.)

Six Nations

At the treaty of Lancaster, in Pennsylvania, about 1774, between the Government of Virginia and the Six Nations, the commissioners from Virginia acquainted the Indians by a speech, that there was at Williamsburg a college with a fund for educating Indian youth; and that if the chiefs of the Six Nations would send down half a dozen of their sons to that college, the government would take care that they be well provided for, and instructed in all the learning of the white people.

The Indians' spokesman replied: "We know that you highly esteem the kind of learning taught in those colleges, and that the maintenance of our young men, while with you, would be very expensive to you. We are convinced, therefore, that you meant to do us good by your proposal and we thank you heartily.

"But you, who are wise, must know that different nations have different conceptions of things; and you will not therefore take it amiss, if our ideas of this kind of education happen not to be the same with yours. We have had some experience of it; several of our young people were formerly brought up at the colleges of the northern provinces; they were instructed in all your sciences; but, when they came back to us, they were bad runners, ignorant of every means of living in the woods, unable to bear either cold or hunger, knew neither how to build a cabin, take a deer, nor kill an enemy, spoke our language imperfectly, were therefore neither fit for hunters, warriors, nor counselors; they were totally good for nothing.

"We are however not the less obligated by your kind offer, though we decline accepting it; and, to show our grateful sense of it, if the gentlemen of Virginia will send us a dozen of their sons, we will take care of their education, instruct them in all we know, and make men of them."

Source: George C. Christensen, "International Curriculum for the Professions," *Phi Kappa Phi Journal*, Fall 1988, p. 28.

While classes in foreign languages, international business and economics, and cultural anthropology are useful to your future in business, the learning still takes place in the classroom, behind campus walls. It is an artificial environment, almost suspended animation, in which few students work for a living and spend much of their time reading books, taking tests, and listening to scholars lecture on various subjects. But most educators realize that much of what students learn in college takes place *outside the classroom*. It takes place in the dormitory room, in the cafeteria, and on the intramural fields. It takes place in a thousand interactions with friends and classmates during the daily life of a typical college student.

The desire to develop your multicultural skills does not come from a classroom lecture or out of a book. Instead, it is based on how you interact with others, *especially others who do not look or behave like you.* According to the Institute of International Education, in 1989 there were more than 25,000 Chinese students attending U.S. colleges and universities, 20,000 Malaysians, 15,000 Canadians, 10,000 Iranians, 6,000 Lebanese, 2,500 Spaniards, and 1,400 Cameroonians. They have come to U.S. colleges to learn. But just as the Indians of the Six Nations so subtly reminded the commissioners of Virginia, they also have much to teach us. Meet them, talk to them, have lunch with them—and learn.

8

The Change Maker

Creative/Innovator Skills Inventory

Face the unknown without fear • Develop a healthy, constructive
nonconformity • Maintain a sense of imagination/curiosity • Be
willing to assume moderate risks • Take responsibility for
successes/failures • Tackle problems with unrepentant optimism •
Develop a strong self-image • Accept change as a challenge •
Overcome the fear of failure • Be willing to see things through

"In the beginning, God created the heaven and the earth" (Genesis
1:1). And so, in the words of the Bible, God was the classic innovator.
He (or She) created something from nothing and in so doing altered
the status quo—the true Change Maker. Creating change is not only
the work of supreme beings, it is a human pursuit as well. Finding
new ways of doing things makes our lives better. It increases our
productivity, efficiency, and effectiveness and the quality of our lives.

Electricity and penicillin, the refrigerator and the elevator, satel-
lites, VCRs, compact disks, and the modern computer chip—the advances are startling. And much of the impetus for change, for a better
life, comes from the private sector—from business. For example,
Squibb Corporation, the huge pharmaceutical company, spent years
and millions of dollars in developing a new class of drug, captopril, to
treat hypertension and congestive heart failure. That is a lifesaving
innovation. Other changes help to solve less critical but nonetheless
important problems in our everyday lives. Consider the problem of
how to keep a 2-year-old boy dry, as told in Lucky Dave, page 134.

Lucky Dave

A recent article by Kenneth Labich, entitled "Innovators," suggests that America's most imaginative companies are turning new ideas into corporate profits. Labich begins his article with a personal observation.

"My older son, now almost 7, was an exceedingly good-natured baby except at bedtime. He required two bulky diapers plus rubber pants to get through the night. He looked and, I suspect, felt quite silly, and even with all that swaddling sometimes suffered from fierce rashes. Poor Paul was born a bit too soon; Procter & Gamble and Kimberly-Clark, leaders in the $5-billion-a-year disposable-diaper market, have been advancing the art and turning out new products at a sizzling pace. My younger son, soon to be 2, tumbles cheerfully into his crib each night wearing a thin, superabsorbent little number able to soak up lakes of whatever. His bottom is rashless, a thing of beauty. Lucky David."

One way or another, thousands of product lines in every type of industry are being transformed. Innovating—creating new products, new services, new ways of turning out goods more cheaply—has become the most urgent concern of corporations everywhere. That is partly because restructuring has left many companies with a few core businesses that are solid but slow growing. Innovation is their best bet for revving things up. In addition, technology has forced the pace of change and sharply cut the effective lifetimes of all kinds of products. Long-playing records sold briskly for decades before cassette tapes posed a serious threat; now compact discs are shaking the market, and a new technology, digital audio tape, is on the way. Innovation is the key and innovators are the key change makers.

Source: Kenneth Labich, "Innovators," *Fortune,* June 6, 1988, p. 51.

The lesson from three new management advice books—*The Pursuit of Innovation, Innovation: The Attacker's Advantage,* and *Innovation and Entrepreneurship*—seems to be that to stand still is to die. Or as MIT professor David Birch, observes, "For every corporation in the U.S., the best predictor of death is stability." Innovation, flexibility, and the ability to change have become necessary business survival skills. But once this is said, the obvious question remains as to how to ensure such innovation. The answer is quite simple.

The best strategy for any company, large or small, that wants to be at the forefront of innovation is to fill the company with innovators: *Find people who embrace change.* It doesn't matter if you're interested in developing a new drug or a new biodegradable diaper. Hire people who are creative and inquisitive. Provide opportunities for people who have imagination and are bored at the thought of doing things "the way they've always been done." These individuals have an excitement about them; they exude energy and are driven by a personal need for discovery. They have vision and an appetite for the unorthodox, and they hate the humdrum. Our society is hailing these people as our new Change Makers.

The cover story in a recent issue of *Hospitals* magazine, for example, was devoted to "Innovators and Entrepreneurs: 1989." The article began: "Meet 13 people who have made a difference. They come from different parts of the country, different types of communities. Some have launched successful businesses. Others have altered health care delivery systems to better serve their communities. Each has taken an innovative approach to a problem and succeeded in solving it." The cover story of the special tenth anniversary issue of *Inc.* magazine was "The Entrepreneur of the Decade." It featured an interview with Steve Jobs, the cofounder of Apple Computer, Inc., and founder of NeXT Computer. All these people have become heroes to the business world.

But let's stop here for a second. The picture we are painting is a bit too rosy. Not everyone is thrilled about the idea of change. Indeed, the notion of change is threatening to many. In fact, it defies a basic law of nature: "Things at rest tend to stay at rest." In a 1989 *New York Times* article entitled "The Challenge of Change," Arthur Schlesinger, the Pulitzer Prize–winning historian and former aide to President John F. Kennedy, comments: "The acceleration of change compels us to perceive life as motion, not as order; the universe not as complete, but as unfinished. The hunger for stability is entirely natural. Change is scary. People instinctively defend the old ways."

The battle over change is fought out every day in every organization in this country. Do we attempt a new approach, a new technology, a new style, or do we stay with the familiar, the comfortable? Change is, indeed, a scary idea to many.

The importance of creative/imaginative skill acquisition for today's college students is largely one of supply and demand. Specifically, today's businesses, especially the large corporations, simply will not survive in this period of rapid change and innovation unless they acquire *creative competence*. We are in an environment in which strong products or services are rendered obsolete or ineffective in a flash. At the same time, such an environment creates daily opportunities for experimentation, for breakthroughs that have an innovative edge.

Large, successful companies have a special need for Change Makers. First, successful companies tend to become complacent and

Get Out Of That Rut

Oscar Wilde said,
"Consistency is
the last refuge of
the unimaginative."
So stop getting up
at 6:05.
Get up at 5:06.
Walk a mile at dawn.
Find a new way
to drive to work.
Switch chores with
your spouse
next Saturday.
Buy a wok.
Study wildflowers.
Stay up alone all night.
Read to the blind.
Start counting
brown-eyed blondes
or blonds.
Subscribe to an
out-of-town paper.
Canoe at midnight.
Don't write to your
congressman,
take a whole scout
troop to see him.
Learn to speak
Italian.
Teach some kid
the thing you do best.
Listen to two hours of
uninterrupted Mozart.
Take up aerobic dancing.
Leap out of that rut.
Savor life.
Remember, we only
pass this way once.

Bally Manufacturing Corporation

Bally Manufacturing Corporation was the largest and most respected builder of slot machines. Its growth was the result of the increased popularity of slot machines and other gaming machines among gamblers and casinos. For example, the number of slot machines in Nevada broke the 100,000 mark in 1986, up almost 40 percent from 1980. But, interestingly, 1986 also brought another landmark. Bally lost its number one position to International Game Technology. Within four years, International Game went from an unprofitable minor player to industry leadership. How? To some extent, the company's success reflects the difficulties that Bally encountered. Industry executives say that Bally was slow to adopt the computer technology that revolutionized gaming machines in the early 1980's, and that the company experienced quality-control problems, giving International Game an opening.

According to Michael Gaughan, the president of the Gold Coast and the Barbary Coast casinos in Las Vegas, "Bally kind of fell asleep."

Source: Richard Stevenson, "Slot Machine Maker Hits Jackpot," *New York Times*, September 12, 1989, p. C1.

---

content. As the old sports adage states, "It is easier to get to the top than it is to stay there." When you are in second place, you're hungry and willing to take risks. (Just look at Avis, Ford, and Apple!) Once you are successful, the natural tendency is to stop experimenting, to stay with what made you number one. You relax.

Bally's story, described above, is nothing new. A review of the list of America's twenty-five largest, most successful corporations over the past sev-enty years shows how fatal success can be. Indeed, GE, USX (formerly US Steel), and Du Pont are the only non-oil-based firms to remain consistently on the list. The others have fallen prey to changing times: dynamic markets, maturing products, and emerging technologies. Success, and the increasing size of a company, tend to have a negative influence on innovation. The larger the business, the higher the prob-ability that its decision making will focus on short-run, internal problems. Getting bigger is almost a universally accepted measure of success. But with the increase in size, there is an accompanying loss of flexibility, adaptability, and simplicity. Rigidity, formalization, and complexity (all characteristics of larger firms) impede innovation and change.

Robert G. Cooper, a UCLA researcher, has carefully studied the ways organizations incorporate change into corporate culture. Cooper discovered that in fifty-six of fifty-eight major commercial innovations that occurred within the past 100 years, the established or then-dominant firm *failed to make the necessary transition to new technologies or innovative practices that would have expanded market opportunities and retained market leadership.* Some examples:

- Gas utilities failed to capitalize on the emerging electrical utility business.

- Manufacturers of mechanical calculators watched on the sidelines as electronic calculators swept the market.

- Vacuum-tube manufacturers refused to enter the transistor business. Instead, they concentrated on making better vacuum tubes.

- Watchmakers, relying on the springs and gears of mechanical watches, missed the opportunity to incorporate digital technology into a new high-fashion market.

In short, these organizations failed to scan the environment for new technologies and innovative practices that would promote organizational interests and corporate goals. Their failure to do so led to new opportunities for new companies to emerge as market innovators and leaders. Indeed, in some cases companies that had a reputation for being market leaders and innovators have failed to *recognize* new technologies, often at great cost. (See Missed Opportunities, page 139.)

Demand for the Change Maker also occurs in smaller companies. As we have mentioned, the real growth in new jobs in the United States has come from small entrepreneurial companies. Entrepreneurship is the creation of organizations, and innovation, or change, is the specific tool of entrepreneurs. It is the means by which they pursue an opportunity in order to create a different business or service. For example, Jon Goodman, director of USC's nationally recognized Entrepreneur Program, says that "undergraduates often start new businesses, while MBA students hope to create new industries."

Smaller companies that operate in specialized-market niches must see change as the norm. Given their size, they cannot afford to have a bunch of bureaucrats slowing things down. They need to be quick and alert. The entrepreneurial companies must search for change, respond to it, and exploit it as an opportunity. That's how they compete successfully against the giants.

Missed Opportunities

Perhaps the most important new product of the 1980s was the microcomputer. It has certainly changed the way students study, faculty members conduct research, and U.S. companies do business. But did you know that three major technology companies *failed* to capitalize on early opportunities that could have dramatically changed the computer business in the 1980s?

Hewlett-Packard, Digital Equipment Corporation (DEC), and Xerox are all top contenders on most lists of the best-managed, most innovative companies in the United States. Yet all three companies missed a key opportunity to enter, perhaps even to define, the microcomputer market because of their inability to change.

- At Hewlett-Packard, product development specialists ignored Steve Wozniak's efforts to demonstrate his prototype of a "micro" computer. Why? Because Wozniak was a technician, not an engineer. Wozniak then teamed up with Steve Jobs to build these small computers. They discovered a market and went on to found Apple Computer!

- DEC founder Kenneth Olsen helped to define the minicomputer market in the early 1970s. A former IBM engineer, Olsen left to start his own company when IBM officials rejected his designs for a computer that was smaller, more specialized, and less expensive than IBM's products. Yet DEC repeatedly missed—some observers say ignored—opportunities to get into the microcomputer market in the early 1980s. Some observers feel that Olsen was unable to change his personal definition of computing, thus handicapping his company at a critical time in the development of a new kind of computer—and an important new computer market.

- Xerox is more than the copier company. It has a tremendous reputation for technology research. Indeed, many of the innovations that helped to define the Macintosh were first conceived and tested in Xerox's research lab in Palo Alto, California. But Xerox could not convert its test systems into successful products.

These companies all have reputations for being innovators; they are frequently cited in management books as being models of organizations that manage well and are forward-thinking. But they were unable to innovate, to scan the environment or to capitalize on opportunities presented by creative employees at a critical juncture in the computer market.

This, then, is the current state of affairs. Large and small, the businesses of the 1990s and the twenty-first century must be on a constant vigil to hire creative, imaginative employees. Let's explore a few of the many ways that today's business student can go about acquiring the skills of the Change Maker.

College and Creativity

Innovation is used by the entrepreneur to develop a new business. It is also used within an existing company to make incremental improvements in products and services. What drives the innovation process? What motivates someone to innovate, to start a new business, or push for a new solution? Undoubtedly, the innovator is a person with a great deal of creativity and imagination. These personal attributes or qualities of the individual influence the way that he or she sees the world. And believe us, creative people do see the world differently.

Perhaps most important, creativity is the ability to think about alternatives. Creative people don't have a limited problem-solution perspective. Instead, they see problems as opportunities. They also don't see just one alternative; they see solutions galore. They are able to *imagine* the possibilities. Imagination is the key that unlocks the door to endless opportunities in life and business. Don't just take our word for it. As Albert Einstein once remarked, "Imagination is more important than knowledge."

In doing the research for this chapter, we reached an inescapable conclusion regarding the Change Maker. Entrepreneurs and innovators with strong creative and imaginative minds are made, not born. Some people believe that the entrepreneurs and innovators of this world have an independence and eagerness to take risks that cannot be taught or learned. They think that creativity and imagination are more a part of your heart and soul than of your mind, that you are born with it and thus can't learn it on a college campus.

But a great deal of evidence suggests otherwise. For example, in 1989 *Inc.* magazine posed questions to many of the founders of some of America's most successful companies. By means of an eight-page survey and dozens of follow-up phone calls, they asked these innovators how they came to create a company. The magazine found that there were few inspired geniuses in the group. Instead, the *Inc.* entrepreneurs were down-to-earth, practical-minded people who used their *experiences,* including college, work, and personal life, to develop a creative mindset. They continually looked for unique opportunities and then pursued them with hard work, drive, and determination. No magic. Just keen eyesight: being able to spot and develop a new idea.

"What I'd really like is a job that doesn't take a lot of time and energy but pays a lot of money so I can be truly creative on my own time."

In addition to the conclusion that innovation is a function of experiences—*learned behavior*—we also found that college students underestimate the market value of creativity skills. In 1986 University of Southwestern Louisiana professors Stephen Payne and Bernard Pettingill compared the results of two surveys—one of managers and the other of management majors in college. Managers were asked to identify those individual qualities most admired in the workplace. Of the eighteen qualities on the list, the top four traits were "responsible," "honest," "capable," and *"imaginative."* Imagination, according to the managers, is a key input to success in the workplace. But what happened when Payne and Pettingill compared the preferences of corporate executives and college students? When the undergraduates were asked the same question, "imagination" came in at a lowly sixteenth place, behind qualities like "cheerful," "helpful," and "forgiving." This sharp difference prompted Payne and Pettingill to conclude: "If management students in college do not perceive the importance of imaginative and creative behavior, college educators must emphasize its demand in business and industry as well as explore new methodologies for trying to develop and reward greater powers of imagination from their students."

Stanford University's Graduate School of Business is perhaps the most visible example of a college that has fostered the acquisition of change-making skills. Two professors, Michael Ray and Rochelle Myers, have developed a course entitled Creativity in Business. The course includes a broad range of lecture topics, exercises, projects, and guest speakers and is one of the most popular in the business program. In fact, it has been so successful that the professors wrote a book based on the course—*Creativity in Business* (New York: Doubleday, 1989)—that is filled with techniques and tools to help managers develop their creative resources.

While there is now a smattering of specific creativity courses in business schools, becoming the Change Maker at most colleges and universities requires a bit of detective work.

The B School

There are several different types of courses within a business program that can foster the development of creativity and imagination in the student. First, there is the course in entrepreneurship. More than 250 (out of several thousand) colleges and universities across the United States have initiated entrepreneurship courses. Whether offering full-fledged programs or just a series of classes, institutions like Babson College, Boston College, Baylor University, and Harvard are taking notice of America's surging small-business climate. These institutions now offer courses and programs centered on the development of new ideas from inspiration to implementation.

The University of Pennsylvania's Wharton School offers a special major in entrepreneurship. Similarly, at the University of Illinois at Chicago, the University of Southern California, and the University of Maryland, entrepreneurship is a concentration within the business program. Table 10 gives a short list of typical course titles.

Other options that the aspiring innovator, or Change Maker, can pursue include independent research, special projects, and honors thesis classes. In general, these are upper-division classes in which students, with a professor's approval, are encouraged to explore a topic of personal interest. There are no exams, textbooks, or structured assignments. The grade is based solely upon the quality of an in-depth examination of an issue. The lack of structure in the course is frightening to many students who have been brought up in a very ordered teaching environment of lectures, studying, exams, and grades. The rewards, however, can be significant. Without a rigid set of dos and don'ts to follow, students are free to exercise their creative energies in searching for a topic, organizing the work and research, and communicating their findings.

Table 10. Courses Emphasizing Development of New Ideas

(selected schools)

Institution	Course Title
University of Illinois at Chicago	New Venture Formation New Product Development
University of Southern California	Management of New Ventures Cases in New Venture Management
The Wharton School	Entrepreneurial Decision Making Venture Initiation
University of Maryland	New Venture Creation Entrepreneurship: Corporate Venturing
---

Finally, a business student should keep his or her eyes open for inspiring, thought-provoking professors, regardless of the course. In virtually every discipline—accounting, operations research, personnel administration, finance, and insurance—you will find professors who demand creative thinking in their classrooms. Such teachers use special projects, exercises, research papers, site visits, and guest lecturers in order to expose students to multiple views. They tend to avoid standard tests, and you'll never see them lecture straight from the textbook. They will challenge you to create, not imitate. They are special people. Seek them out.

The Creative Arts

Recent scientific research shows that the two hemispheres of the human brain process different kinds of information and handle different tasks and problems. The left hemisphere specializes in the analytical reasoning process discussed in Chapter 6, The Problem Solver, while the right hemisphere is associated primarily with those activities that we consider creative. (See Table 11.) The left-brain thinker uses convergent thinking (one conclusion or alternative), is rational, and bases a conclusion on facts and reasoning. The right-brain thinker, in contrast, uses divergent thinking (many conclusions or

Table 11. Comparison of Left- and Right-Hemisphere Functions

Left Mode

Logical, analytical, sequential, linear—drawing conclusions based on logical order of things; figuring things out in a sequential order, step-by-step, part-by-part, one element after another, in an ordered way.

Right Mode

Intuitive, nonlinear—multiple processing of information; utilizing intuitive feeling of how things fit, belong, or go together, making leaps of insight based upon hunches, feelings, incomplete data, patterns, imagery.

Source: Eugene Raudsepp, *How Creative Are You?* New York: Pedigree, 1981.

alternatives) and is nonrational; his or her intuition plays a more important role than reason or facts.

Understandably, college students, especially business students, overdevelop their left hemisphere. As noted, many college courses have a lecture format. The professor talks for an hour, and the student writes it down. The student also has an assigned textbook. Several times each term the professor gives an examination on the material covered in the textbook and lectures. There is little imagination involved in the process. Grades are based upon the student's ability to regurgitate data.

Business classes are especially slanted toward this approach to learning. A professor in a cost-accounting course feels that his or her first obligation is to teach a set of tools. A finance professor wants to help the student understand a series of financial techniques. In both instances, the knowledge the student receives is critical in getting a desirable job; however, the learning "process" often leaves little room for imagination and creativity. The student is rewarded for repeating the procedure as it was taught, not for questioning its relevance or attempting to find a new and possibly better way to approach the subject.

There are, however, numerous courses in college that are concerned with creativity and imagination, the skills that fuel the visual, experimental side of the Change Maker. For example, studio art courses are long on creation and short on imitation. Painting, drawing, sculpture, and photography courses encourage students to express themselves in many ways. There is no single truth, no single way of doing something. Many different configurations or combinations of ideas work equally well. Students are challenged to look, listen, touch, and feel—to explore, to create change.

SNAPSHOTS

Gisela Voss was a marketing major in college. But to balance out a steady diet of accounting, finance, statistics, and marketing courses, she also took courses in the arts—drawing, painting, and printmaking. One of her most rewarding courses was creative writing. According to Gisela, the professor had a few techniques to get the creative juices flowing: "We had a small class of maybe twelve people. The professor used to assign us a role, say a food critic, and you'd go to a restaurant, have a meal, and then write a review for the class. Another person would have to rent a movie and write a movie review. Then we'd spend time in class critiquing each other's articles. It really taught me to expand the way that I look at things."

After graduating from college with a marketing major and art minor, Gisela took a marketing research position at Hasbro, the toy company that makes Mr. Potato Head, G.I. Joe, and Tinker Toys. "My creative side really got a workout. You have a set of research techniques that you typically use to interview consumers, but you can imagine that they don't work very well with a 4-year-old. For example, you can't just ask little kids if they like a new product. It just doesn't work like it does with adults. One of the things I started doing was to have the kids bring in their favorite toy from home. Then I'd ask them whether or not they would trade their favorite toy for the new one, the prototype that we were thinking of developing. You really knew you had a hot product if kids would give up their favorite toy."

In this case the blend of right-brain and left-brain abilities proved to be a winning—*and balanced*—combination. As Gisela notes, "Virtually every standard marketing research technique that you learned in college ends up having to be creatively adapted to the situation. Knowing the techniques, and the standard step-by-step process, isn't enough. You have to be flexible and learn to adjust to a different set of circumstances." Gisela took this flexibility and right-left brain duality to another job that capitalizes on her abilities as a Change Maker. Today, Gisela develops and markets toys for the Museum of Fine Arts in Boston. All the courses she took in the arts and business now come to life *together* as she walks by a silk robe from the Ming Dynasty and designs a kite out of it or adapts a squiggle on a Miro painting to be a baby's rattle.

Another place to exercise the left brain is the English department. At most colleges and universities the English department offers courses in creative or fiction writing. Such courses require the student to explore his or her own imagination and create new patterns of thought. And whether you are a finance major working at the Federal Reserve Board or a marketing major employed by the Museum of Fine Arts in Boston (read the story of Gisela Voss on page 145), such patterns help to create exciting possibilities in the world of business.

Campus Profile
Ball State University

In 1918 the Ball brothers, of a prominent Muncie, Indiana, industrial family, donated to the state the campus of the Muncie Normal Institute. Today, Ball State University is a comprehensive publicly assisted institution located on a 955-acre campus in a city of 80,000 people. Muncie is an average-sized city for Indiana, but Ball State, with almost 20,000 students, 34 residence halls, approximately 300 student organizations, and 33 national social fraternities and sororities, is well above the national average in size.

Ball State offers 140 majors and minors through six colleges: applied sciences and technology, architecture and planning, business, education, fine arts, and sciences and humanities. Twelve required courses for business students provide an extensive "common body of knowledge" in business information systems, principles of business law, business policy, and strategic management. In addition, students take courses in their major, as well as a set number of general education courses.

Ball State has a complete eight-course sequence in its Entrepreneurship/Small-Business Management Program, which was started in 1983. The coordinator, Dr. Donald Kuratko, sees the program as unique: "It does more than teach from a book. Students are challenged to teach themselves, so they enter the business world with the confidence to do things they never believed they could do." Kuratko says the program, which has earned two national awards, makes Ball State business graduates more appealing to the business industry: "Employers are looking for more entrepreneurship-minded employees, employees who are creative and thinking of the future."

While there are probably dozens of courses that could aid the Change Maker in skill acquisition, we suggest the following.

Business

Entrepreneurship: Development and management of an entrepreneurial organization including pre-start-up, survival, growth, and the transition from entrepreneurial to professional management.

New Venture Creation: Advanced small-business entrepreneurship. Requires a thorough research project culminating in the development of a finished plan for a small-business venture, to be approved by an outside board of professional experts.

Independent Study: Supervised study of some phase of management. May consist of an experiment, library research, or an analysis of current management practices and methods.

Fine Arts

Photography: Introduction to photography as an expressive art form, with emphasis on the development of photographic vision as well as technical proficiency.

Drawing: The application of basic principles and elements of art as they relate to drawing concepts. Emphasis is on the development of perceptual awareness and familiarity with a broad range of media and techniques.

Creative Writing Workshop: The fundamentals of the short story, such as the use of language, image, and structure. Emphasis on the student's ability to write clearly and dramatically.

Understanding Failure

There is one aspect of this subject that we have purposefully put off until now. Perhaps the most important part of the education of the Change Maker is to understand the importance of failure. Most courses in business are, as we have noted, left-brain dominated: "logical, analytical, sequential, linear." The list of left-brain-oriented subjects studied in business courses is exhaustive: the analysis of a balance sheet or income statement in accounting, the capital asset pricing model in finance, regression analysis in statistics, and locational analysis in retailing. These are the tools and techniques of businesspeople.

The problem lies in the learning and the application of these tools. In the classroom the professor assigns a chapter in a book and then takes several days reviewing the techniques and possibly giving some problems as assignments. Then comes the big day—the examination. You are expected to be able to read a problem, choose the appropriate technique, apply it correctly, and derive the one right solution. There is little or no room for ambiguity or interpretation in the process. Partial credit is hardly ever given. Either you get the answer or you don't. Either you succeed or you fail.

In many aspects of business, however, success and failure are not so easily categorized. Should we always see failure as the worst possible condition? And if we make success so important, will it inhibit our desire to try anything that doesn't virtually *guarantee* success? Perhaps success and failure are not exact opposites. Perhaps in some situations they are very closely related. An enlightening story about one "successful" inventor may show a different relationship.

> *When Thomas Edison was intent upon creating incandescent light, he went through more than 9,000 experiments in an attempt to produce the bulb. Finally, one of his associates walked up to him and asked, "Why do you persist in this folly? You have failed more than 9,000 times." Edison looked at him incredulously and said, "I haven't even failed once; 9,000 times I've learned what doesn't work."*

We don't have to look to history to provide us with examples of the importance of failure as it relates to success. We began this chapter by saying that the twenty-first-century company will have to innovate and change—to stand still in the business environment is and will continue to be deadly. Innovation is the medicine for the disease of inaction. But innovation and change necessarily entail uncertainty. This uncertainty or risk must be embraced so that success can be achieved through repeated failure and *introspection*. Like Thomas Edison, you learn from each failure. But a company or an individual that is unwilling to make mistakes is not going to go anywhere. As management guru Tom Peters comments in *Thriving on Chaos*, "If you are trying new things, failure is, at times, inevitable. So you have to have an atmosphere where people can make mistakes—knowing, of course, that there is something to learn from each and every failure." (See Failure 101 on page 149.)

In college, therefore, you need to seek out situations where failure is tolerated, even encouraged. Maybe it's in a creative writing class or via contact with a business professor who will be your adviser for an independent study project. Maybe your school has a Failure 101–type course. Push yourself—force yourself into a position where you can take some chances, where 100 percent of the grade is not based upon a final exam.

The Change Maker, a valuable asset in any business today, is the person who is willing to assume some risk in order to create new opportunities. It is the person who realizes that almost every area of business innovation has had its history of failures (learning situations) that ultimately led to success. For in reality, the greatest failure is failing to attempt a new idea at all. Or as Chester Barnard, former president of the New Jersey Telephone Company and the Rockefeller Foundation, once remarked, "To try and fail is at least to learn. To fail to try is to suffer the inestimable loss of what might have been."

Failure 101

Walking into an engineering class at the University of Houston, a professor and his guest are greeted by students making the thumbs-down gesture and singing out a chorus of "boos." The professor, wearing a World War I combat helmet and a T-shirt that pictures a two-legged chair with the word "Failure" written above it, is pleased.

In this class, officially called Innovation Design for Civil Engineers but known by students as Failure 101, those are signs of approval, even affection. "It's all part of the opposite mentality I'm trying to foster," says the professor, Jack V. Matson, who says he wears Mickey Mouse ears or headgear like the combat helmet to illustrate to his students the importance of spontaneity and serendipity. "We are taught all our lives that only success counts, but we have to recognize the role of failure in the learning and creativity processes, too."

Mr. Matson has been teaching the innovation design course with an accent on failure to undergraduate and graduate engineering students at Houston since 1983. Last year, he took time off to teach a similar course in risk taking and failure in entrepreneurship to business students at the University of Michigan. In both courses, students are required to create a consumer product or service and market it. He encourages his students to consider and try many different products, designs, and marketing strategies before they settle on their final project.

By celebrating failure, Mr. Matson says, he is encouraging students to take risks and be creative. Failure also helps to define weaknesses, he says, and motivates people toward success. "I'm not an advocate of failure for its own sake," the professor says, "but there is something that I call intelligent failure that provides the building blocks for success."

Source: Adapted from Debra Blum, *The Chronicle of Higher Education,* April 11, 1990. Reprinted with permission, © 1990.

9

The Twenty-first-Century Leader

Leadership Skills Inventory

Be able to articulate a vision • Show a willingness to accept responsibility • Understand followers and their needs • Demonstrate the need/drive to achieve • Be capable of motivating others • Accept and learn from criticism • Be able to identify critical issues • Use tact, diplomacy, and discretion • Be able to act decisively • Behave confidently and courageously

Japan has emerged as one of the world's great economic powers over the past two decades. Smaller in size than the state of California, Japan has virtually no natural resources. It imports almost all the raw materials that its factories turn into cars, VCRs, TVs, computer chips, and electronic goods. Although Japan is geographically isolated from major markets in Europe and North America, people across the globe clamor for Japanese goods. The nation that once had a reputation for low-quality, inexpensive products is now known throughout the world for top-quality manufacturing processes and high-quality products. How is this possible?

Let's look at one industry for a clue. Every day it becomes clearer that the Japanese are on their way to world domination in the business of semiconductors, the central processing units and memory chips essential for computers and the growing number of consumer electronic products, from microwave ovens to CD players. When National Semiconductor Corporation terminated its chip-manufacturing unit in 1989, only three U.S. companies remained in this critical business. Indeed, the U.S. share of the worldwide computer chip market has fallen in the past decade from 60 percent to less than 20 percent.

The semiconductor business is no fluke. It is going the way of others—consumer electronics, steel, automotive products, and machine tools. Why? Is it because Japan provides better education for its people, spends more money on research and development (R&D), and secures more patents in high technology than do Europe and the United States combined? Well, those are certainly key explanations. But there is an even more basic reason. Daniel Queyssac, president and CEO of SGS-Thomson Microelectronics, Inc., recently concluded in an issue of *Industry Week* that the reason for America's continuing slide in the semiconductor market is clear: "We brought all this upon ourselves. Leadership is the reason for the U.S. decline. Our industrial leaders are no longer best." Queyssac does not speak alone. Peter Drucker, America's foremost authority on management, has concluded that "Leadership in management—not technological innovation—made Japan a great economic power."

We are losing the *economic race* because we are losing the *leadership race*. Other countries—Japan, Korea, West Germany, Holland, and Sweden—are developing leaders who understand quality and efficiency and can rally a work force to produce better and better goods of all kinds. These leaders are willing to take the risk and assume the responsibility of leadership. They are competent in their jobs; they foster enthusiasm among their workers and great trust for high-quality products among their customers. They have a clear picture of what needs to be achieved and realize that it takes people, lots of people working together, to get there. They delegate and reward others for superior efforts. In short, they lead. Jan Carlzon, president of Stockholm-based SAS, explains his personal "leadership" philosophy in Helicopter Sense. (See page 153.)

The leadership gap has not gone unnoticed in this country. Indeed, within the past few years U.S. companies have responded aggressively by developing in-house training programs and sending individuals to leadership seminars. The Center for Creative Leadership in Greensboro, North Carolina, for example, has 200 people on staff, conducts programs for individual participants, and does contract work for organizations. In 1989 the center conducted leadership seminars for senior managers from Goodyear Tire and Rubber, Eastman Kodak, and Ford. According to center psychologist David Campbell, "Leadership has become the universal vitamin C pill. Everyone seems to want megadoses of it."

Other companies, for instance, General Motors, have developed their own programs. GM has invested $3 million–plus in a program

Helicopter Sense

I am the president of a large airline, but I can neither fly a plane nor repair one—and no one at SAS expects me to. A leader today must have much more general qualities: good business sense and a broad understanding of how things fit together—the relationships among individuals and groups inside and outside the company and the interplay among the various elements of the company's operations.

What is required is strategic thinking, or "helicopter sense"—a talent for rising above the details to see the lay of the land. The ability to understand and direct change is crucial for effective leadership. Today's business leader must manage not only finances, production, technology, and the like but also human resources. By defining clear goals and strategies and then communicating them to his employees and training them to take responsibility for reaching those goals, the leader can create a secure working environment that fosters flexibility and innovation.

Thus, the new leader is a listener, communicator, and educator—an emotionally expressive and inspiring person who can create the right atmosphere rather than make all the decisions himself.

Source: Jan Carlzon, *Moments of Truth,* Cambridge, Mass.: Ballinger Publishing Company, 1987.

---

called Leadership Now. General Foods has developed a five-phase executive leadership program that is spread over an eighteen-month period, taking up about twenty-five days. Its primary purpose is to "promote individual growth, development, general broadening, and foster the ability to appreciate and make the most of diversity." Weyerhaeuser has decided to get on the leadership bandwagon as well. (See page 154.)

Wanted: Leaders Who Can— and Will—Make a Difference

Leadership used to be optional. A few key people in a company had to provide overall corporate direction while the day-to-day operations were handled by a staff who managed quality control—and decided

Making Things Happen at Weyerhaeuser

Changing the company is the aim of a management education program at Weyerhaeuser, the huge wood and paper products company located in Tacoma, Washington. "If you learn anything as a result of the sessions at the Weyerhaeuser Leadership Institute, it should be to step out and take risks," says Charley Bingham, Weyerhaeuser executive vice president. "Make something happen."

Crisis Management. To be taken by 400 managers, the course is described as one of the largest and most comprehensive in the country. It begins with an outdoor crisis simulation session. In one exercise . . . a group of managers had to raise a barrel of unknown and untouchable toxic waste uphill. "I was a little confused at first about what the outdoor exercises had to do with making wood products," says Ron Endicott, manager of a sawmill in Philadelphia, Mississippi. "But it broke down leadership into elements you can nail right to the wall—this is what happens, and this is what to do about it."

Customers Attend. Four months after the first session, the class met again for an intense 5 1/2 days of marketing fundamentals. Four to six customers are invited to attend these sessions. This is intended to share their perceptions of the company firsthand while learning what it means to develop long-term partnerships between suppliers and customers. "It helps to have backup from Weyerhaeuser in conveying a quality image to our customers," says Wallace Poole, sales manager for Pool Lumber Company, Covington, Louisiana.

Creativity. During the third week the emphasis is on increasing creativity on the job, both personally and within each business unit. Participants acted out problem-solving scenarios and later analyzed how well they handled the situation. Simultaneously, each manager received feedback collected earlier from coworkers back home. A consultant coordinated private sessions with each manager in this delicate portion of the training as managers heard how well their colleagues rated their leadership skills.

Tying It Together. Finally, the group of managers return for a fourth week of sessions. Through a complex computer simulation, the participants will run their own businesses, putting into practice what they've learned about leadership, marketing, and creativity. "Strong leadership, understanding our markets and our customers, a culture that sustains this drive—these are the things that will make the difference," Mr. Bingham says. "The institute is designed to accelerate the progress we're already making."

Source: Adapted from Lad Kuzela, *Industry Week,* August 24, 1987, p. 26. Reprinted with permission. *Industry Week* © Penton Publishing.

just "how good" products should be. In the relatively stable and prosperous 1950s and 1960s lots of leadership was rarely necessary. Indeed, too much leadership could actually create problems by disrupting established routines—"If it ain't broke, don't fix it." *What has changed?* What has pushed leadership from the bottom of the skills inventory list to a place at the top, making it one of the qualities most sought in today's business professionals? A fundamental shift in the business environment is responsible.

This shift reflects a dramatic increase in competitive intensity. Let's look at some examples.

- *Automobiles.* Used to be that the automobile industry in the United States was dominated by the Big Three: General Motors, Ford, and Chrysler. Then the Japanese penetrated the low end of the car market with Honda, Toyota, and Nissan, and the Europeans attacked the luxury part of the market with BMW and Mercedes Benz. Now Japanese car plants are the major source of new jobs in the domestic auto industry. In California, imported cars account for over half the car market.

- *Banking.* Used to be that banking was a stable business. Banks handled checking and commercial transactions while savings and loan associations (S&Ls) were the place you put your savings and got a home mortgage. Then S&Ls started handling checking accounts, and other players got into the banking business. Suddenly the competition is Sears, Merrill Lynch, American Express, and Japanese banks. Ford, General Motors, and General Electric are in the consumer lending business, and AT&T now issues consumer credit cards just like VISA, MasterCard, and American Express.

- *Hospitals.* A hospital used to be the only place you would go for surgery, major or minor. Today, a growing number of surgical procedures are performed at outpatient clinics, often far away from traditional hospital facilities. These outpatient surgical clinics charge less, and patients go home on the day of surgery. The competition from these new forms of health-care centers has affected the way traditional hospitals do business.

- *Colleges.* Historically, colleges had a kind of gentlemen's agreement about competition: It was generally kept to the athletic field. Today, because of the demographic shifts affecting the nation, colleges are competing for students to maintain their enrollments. In addition to new brochures touting their campus as a wonderful place for your education, colleges are also offering new academic programs and better support services. Indeed, whatever complaints you may have about classes, food service, or other aspects of your college experience, be assured that things are much better, more student sensitive, than they were twenty years ago. College administrators realize that their financial health depends on enrollment, on student decisions to enroll and to stay enrolled. The competition for enrollment has made them increasingly sensitive to their primary clientele: students.

Autos, banks, health care, even higher education—in industry after industry and sector after sector the basic pattern is the same: Boundaries are changing, new players are making "old" stable markets increasingly more competitive. *And the competition will continue to increase.* As one perceptive officer in a major U.S. corporation noted in John Kotter's recent book *The Leadership Factor:*

> *It was a whole lot easier to be an executive thirty years ago. Back then, there were lots of opportunities for growth. Today, there is more competition and our markets are much more mature. When I first joined the company in 1952, we actually had monthly "allocation meetings" in our division, meetings in which we decided which customer got our products. Can you believe that? Today, we need more and better leaders than back then, broad people with vision and self-confidence. Without these people, there is no way we will continue to prosper. In some of our businesses, without them we won't even survive.*

Most business organizations have not prepared for this kind of turbulent economic environment. They continue to find and develop leadership in the same ways they did during stable economic times. But intense competition has forced companies to move faster to bring products to market, to be more flexible in changing to meet a quickly evolving environment, and to be more efficient and cost-effective in responding to shrinking profit levels. Hit-or-miss leadership at the highest echelons of a company—not every company is led by a Jan Carlzon—is no longer sufficient. More and more, leadership cannot be defined simply as a "vision" forged by a handful of executives; it is a broad-based skill required of people at all levels of the organization.

As shown in the first chapter of this book, the new organizational structure that characterizes successful companies in the 1990s is flatter, less hierarchical. These companies are decentralized, with responsibility delegated to those who until now have composed the order-obeying bottom level of the pyramid. The responsibility for day-to-day decision making has to reside with the people who create and market a product or service. Responsibility, control, and leadership must exist at the level of the assembly line worker, the bank teller, the airline flight attendant, and the fork lift operator—the people on the front lines. It makes sense to empower the people who are closest to the action. In the game of soccer, for example, the owner is a leader whose job it is to put together the best team, to select the right players. On the field there is a team captain, similar to a manager in business, with the authority to choose plays and issue orders during the course of the game—another leader. But most important are the individual players, each of whom must assume responsibility for his or her own actions once the game begins. Imagine a situation in which a soccer player breaks away toward an open goal and suddenly abandons the ball to run over to the sidelines and ask the coach—as the "leader"—for the order to kick the ball into the goal. Before the player can run back to the ball, he or she has lost not only the ball but perhaps also the game.

In the new supercompetitive business environment we have described, you can't wield total control from the top of a pyramid; nor for that matter can you control the action from the sidelines. You must give authority to individuals throughout the organization. They are the ones who can sense changes in a dynamic market. They are the ones who can respond quickly. They are the ones who will have to become leaders.

While the need for leaders in the twenty-first century seems clear, the answers to a number of fundamental leadership questions are not so clear. First, is there any fundamental difference between leaders and managers? The answer appears to be yes and no. Yes, there is a difference, but in a modern organization an extensive overlap of managing and leading qualities is needed in the same people. Management is basically a process whose function is to produce *consistent* results in critical areas. Indeed, if we define management as the administrative ordering of things, with written plans, well-documented annual objectives, clear organizational charts, frequent reports, detailed and precise position descriptions, and regular performance evaluations against objectives, then many of our companies are reasonably well managed. But well led? These same companies may excel in the ability to handle all the routine inputs each day, but they may never ask whether the routine should be done at all.

Leadership is a process whose function is to produce change. Typically, leadership involves creating a vision of the future and a strategy for achieving that vision. It involves communicating that direction to everyone so that all understand it and believe it. It also entails providing an environment that will inspire and motivate people to overcome obstacles. In this way, leadership produces change. According to USC professor Warren Bennis, a leading researcher in the area of leader-

SNAPSHOTS

Rhonda Beran, a marketing and psychology graduate from the University of Oregon, began working for the San Francisco–based Computer Resource Group, Inc. (CRG), in 1988 as the marketing coordinator. The company was founded over twenty years ago as a recruiting and placement firm specializing in the computer industry. The original two-man company has grown to sixty employees, with annual sales approaching $25 million. CRG has also expanded other ways. It now has five divisions providing a host of services to the computer industry, its largest source of revenue coming from computer consulting services provided on a contract basis.

In 1987 the company faced limited opportunities for enlarging the revenue margins on contract consulting services, coupled with increased competition. The decision was made to begin developing new products. After a year and a half of research and development, CRG introduced the Information Systems Series, designed to facilitate documenting standards and procedures for corporate computer centers.

The problem that CRG faced, however, was that while it had developed a solid product, it was a regional service firm, not a national product firm. The managers had only a limited understanding of marketing, little experience in advertising and public relations, and no knowledge of distribution channels. They also did not have the resources to hire a vice president of marketing with experience in the computer products industry, so the implementation of this new national venture was given to the recently hired marketing coordinator. According to Rhonda, "The problem was never with the product. The individual at CRG who developed the product did so based on her own documentation experience as a computer consultant. But we weren't IBM. We didn't have any brand familiarity. Nobody outside of the Bay Area had ever heard of us. I had to get smart fast."

She went to libraries and conferences and arranged meetings with industry experts. She put together a series of marketing research projects and examined the media kits from leading computer industry journals. She did economic studies of various industries that used computers. "We didn't have a guide to follow. We'd never done this before. I had never done this before. They sure didn't teach me in college how to roll out a national product. And we did make mistakes. But in spite of that, we have been successful. It just took a willingness to take a risk, and a group of people who were committed to making the idea a reality."

ship, "Managers are people who do things right; leaders are people who do the right thing." Both roles are crucial, but they differ profoundly. Leaders must be managers, but managers are not necessarily leaders. Perhaps most important, people seek leadership. People don't want to be managed; they want to be led.

The second question follows from the first. Since leadership differs from management and is much desired in U.S. industry, can leadership be taught? There is a tendency among some to equate charisma with leadership. No doubt, leaders such as John F. Kennedy and Martin Luther King Jr. were born with a certain gift. But leadership researchers seem to agree that much of effective leadership is plain hard work. For example, Morgan McCall, a senior research scientist at the Center for Effective Organizations at the University of Southern California, draws an analogy to classical pianists: "Some great talents are born; they have an edge. But they work, work, work. They have a gift, but they practice 4 or 6 hours a day." The foundation of effective leadership is thinking through a unit's mission, defining it, and establishing it clearly and visibly. Also, effective and successful leaders see leadership as responsibility rather than as rank and privilege. Finally, an effective leader is one who understands the importance of trust and works to earn it from others. These are the building blocks of leadership, *and they can be taught.*

On Becoming a Leader

You may be asking yourself at this point, "Well, what does all this have to do with me?" To a high school senior or a college freshman or sophomore, a discussion of leadership at General Foods, General Motors, and Weyerhaeuser may seem pretty heady stuff. Perhaps you don't see yourself in the same league as past presidents, world leaders, or the heads of major corporations. Perhaps you're thinking, "So why should I care? I'm just trying to get a college degree, and then a job would be nice." If so, maybe a bit of recent research will give you the proper perspective.

In *The Leadership Factor,* John Kotter discusses the results of his research, identifying the firms with the best reputations for quality of management and ability to attract, keep, and develop talented people. These companies include IBM, Hewlett-Packard, 3M, Morgan Guaranty Bank, Boeing, Citicorp, Du Pont, and Delta Airlines. Kotter explores why these companies are unique and concludes that, along with other practices, they do a "superior job of recruiting people with leadership potential." Morgan Guaranty International Bank, for example, asks everyone who interviews candidates to fill out a one-page form, "Prospective Employee—Interview Evaluation." The form carefully cautions the interviewers to keep in mind four factors that have little to do with technical components of banking; one of those factors is leadership potential.

"With all the well-educated and talented people we hire," one of the bankers notes, "you'd think we would be guaranteed plenty of leadership and management potential. But it's not true. Unless we focus on that explicitly, we end up with a lot of smart technicians who often lack common sense and basic interpersonal skills." So, in fact, not only does industry want leadership skills, but corporate executives and small-business owners are becoming more inspired about finding it. They realize that they can no longer wait for a talented junior executive, an energetic research analyst, or an enthusiastic sales representative to emerge from the pack. They are aggressively searching college campuses for graduates who show the vital signs of leadership potential, qualities required *at all levels* if their companies are to be successful in the twenty-first century.

But don't think that the task of acquiring leadership skills while you are in college will be easy. No department of a college, no academic discipline, exclusively deals with the field of leadership. Colleges are better geared to turning out academics, intellectuals, managers, and technicians than they are to producing genuine leaders. Issues that relate to leadership, however, can be found tucked away in many different areas of a college or university. For example, social psychologists have a long tradition of serious concern about the connection between the individual leader and the organizational culture. The essence of political science is the study of leader-follower interaction in the larger society. Sociologists look at the emergence and behavior of leaders in small groups, and historians have been writing about leaders down through the ages. Communications often deals with the nature of the interaction between leaders and followers. Philosophy is interested in connecting the action of leaders to a set of moral principles, and management focuses on the effects of leadership on corporate performance.

In addition to these scattered offerings, many colleges and universities offer specific courses or programs on the subject of leadership. Most often, these courses or programs are developed and administered through the office of student affairs, as opposed to an academic discipline. For example, student organizations and groups are the vehicles for the Leadership Development Program at the University of Vermont. Russell Baumhover, coordinator of the program, believes its goal is to nurture leadership skills. "Everyone," says Baumhover, "has the potential to be a leader. Through involvement in student groups and activities, students can become aware of their leadership skills."

Two courses, one an introduction to leadership, the other an advanced seminar, are offered through the program. The introductory course, Leadership: Theories, Styles, and Realities, is limited to fifty students and has two components: In the first half students discuss their notion of leadership; in the second they analyze different aspects of leadership, for example, power, authority, and motivation. Students who successfully complete the introductory class are eligible to take the advanced seminar in leadership. There, students are challenged to look beyond their immediate environment and to study the concept of leadership from a more philosophical perspective. Required readings include John F. Kennedy's *Profiles in Courage* and *Habits of the Heart*, by Robert Bellah and his associates at the University of California at Berkeley.

There is also an Emerging Leader Program at the University of Vermont. Each year it helps thirty first-year students nominated for the program to identify and develop their leadership skills. Activities include a series of weekend retreats, group exercises, seminars, monthly meetings, and dinners with the president and dean of students.

Educators at North Carolina's Davidson College first became interested in providing students with leadership training way back in 1967. What has evolved over the past twenty-plus years is the North Carolina Fellows Program. The program is open to all sophomores; the single prerequisite is that students must participate in six of eight seminar/training sessions. The sessions focus on skills necessary to all modes of leadership: time management, motivation and productivity, personal communication styles, and the ability to conduct meetings. In addition to an annual two-day retreat, the program includes the opportunity to carry out a summer internship.

The University of San Diego has taken a different approach to leadership. As we noted, most leadership courses and programs are attached to student affairs, as opposed to any specific academic discipline. But in 1984 the University of San Diego established an 18-credit-hour leadership minor for undergraduates. The minor was a natural outgrowth of the School of Education's doctoral program in educational leadership. At the core of the program are four courses: Leadership in Organizations, Leadership in Groups, Leadership: Practical Experience, and Leadership Seminar. The first two courses provide a strong basis for understanding how leadership transforms organizations and groups. In their junior year, students participate in a semester-long internship that enables them to observe "leaders" in an active setting. The senior-level Leadership Seminar highlights the minor, providing a forum for students to discuss contemporary issues in leadership. According to William Foster, associate professor in the Division of Leadership and Administration, the focus of the program is a firm belief that *"every* student can exert leadership in some capacity."

The business student has no greater access to courses or experiences that develop leadership skills than does any other major. Few, if any, schools offer leadership courses as part of the business curriculum. Some professors will explore the topic in an organizational behavior course. Additionally, any course or extracurricular activity that allows you to work in small groups is a great way to begin to test your own leadership potential. (Extracurricular activities are discussed in Chapter 10.)

We need to note, however, how critical it is to seek out these opportunities. We know of no required leadership courses in any business school program. Indeed, while leadership skills are being sought by industry, numerous critics suggest that colleges do a poor job of developing those skills in undergraduates. In a recent article Ed Wheeler, dean of community life at Oglethorpe University, argues that college is a place to cultivate enlightened leadership: "It is that fertile ground on which we can encourage and develop future leaders, people of intellect who will help to chart passage over the course confronting us—a path of challenges, terror, and complexity." But, as Wheeler goes on to observe, "Modern colleges, however, get low marks in the achievement of that objective."

Kenneth E. Clark, a senior scientist with the Center for Creative Leadership, has made a more direct observation. According to Clark, although college presidents emphasize leadership and talk a lot about the role of their institution in preparing students to accept their civic responsibilities, "rarely do they play their own leadership role in encouraging additions to the curriculum to accomplish these objectives." In the classrooms "faculty teach what they know, and they know very little about leadership. They gave up a life of action to join the ivory tower. For faculty to act to change society is not natural." As a result, he says, at most colleges "there are very few course experiences offered as part of the undergraduate curriculum that aim to develop leadership qualities."

The training of the Twenty-first-Century Leader is in your hands, and you must deliberately acquire and practice leadership skills while in college. The opportunities won't be handed to you; you'll have to find them. However, many colleges are eager to help you. Some 600 campuses across the United States have some type of leadership development program. These programs often include both academic and extracurricular components, plus options for on- and off-campus internships. Their goal is to help cultivate leaders who will make a difference—in college and later in life when they assume their roles in corporations and communities across the country.

Campus Profile
The College of Wooster

The College of Wooster is generally typical of the hundreds of small four-year liberal arts colleges that dot the landscape of this country. Founded in 1866, it is located about 50 miles south of Cleveland, is affiliated with the Presbyterian Church, and maintains selective admissions policies. It is a community of fewer than 2,000 students, faculty members, and administrators.

However, the college is somewhat atypical during the freshman and senior years. All freshmen are required to complete a seminar program that stresses critical thinking and critical writing. In their senior year, students spend two semesters working on a major investigative or creative project that culminates in the writing of a thesis or the production of a substantial creative work. A one-on-one tutorial with a faculty member is an integral part of the senior independent study program.

As in most smaller liberal arts colleges, students who want to study business get a healthy dose of economics. Indeed, the Department of Economics offers two majors, economics and business economics. The major in business economics is designed to provide a course of study within the context of the liberal arts for "those students who plan careers in business immediately after graduation." According to Wooster's catalog, "The requirements of the major are formulated in such a way as to acquaint the student with the structure and organization of the business firm, while at the same time providing a framework of theoretical and quantitative analysis so that the student is better able to understand the decision-making process within the firm in the context of our society."

Administrators at Wooster believe that there is a fundamental link between the liberal arts and leadership. The college catalog states: "From their origin the liberal arts have been the essential preparation for the professions and for roles of leadership in society." But leadership and the study of leadership are two different issues. "Leadership is a legitimate area of intellectual inquiry that is little examined," says Donald Harward, vice president for academic affairs at the College of Wooster. "We have an obligation to turn a critical light on the topic and explore what leadership in society means, even though it doesn't neatly fit into the curriculum." Of particular interest to the Wooster student who is interested in acquiring the skills of the Twenty-first-Century Leader is an interdepartmental course, Leadership Theory and Practice, taught by twelve faculty members and including twice-weekly seminars in which students, through readings and films, confront the question "What is leadership?" Their readings include Plato's *The Republic,* Machiavelli's *The Prince,* Thomas Hardy's *The Mayor of Casterbridge,* and biographies of Lee Iacocca and Martin Luther King Jr., among other contemporary books.

Leadership study at the College of Wooster, therefore, might include the following.

Leadership Theory and Practice: A study of significant theories on leadership and the applicability of theories to accounts of leadership, past and present. Special emphasis on diverse cultural contexts, global interdependence, and consequences of leadership.

Complex Organizations: An introduction to understanding large organizations and behavior within them. Emphasis will be placed on individual adaptation in organizations and the structural characteristics in organizations. Forces and programs bringing about changes in organizations will also be examined from the perspective of the leaders of change.

Group Communication: Form, content, and consequences of communication within groups. The focus of this course is group communicative behavior and the dynamics of group process. Topics include communication aspects, such as communication skills and participation, group discussion, problem solving in groups, group leadership, and evaluation of group performance.

Finally, we should repeat an aspect of the study of leadership that may be obvious by now. It is a useful art, and, as such, it must be practiced. Reading about it is one thing; doing it is something else again. There are many opportunities on a college campus like Wooster's to become involved in activities where leadership skills are required, for example, student government. (We will explore life outside the classroom in the next chapter.)

The Ten Commandments of Leadership

U.S. businesses desperately need better leadership. Companies that will be successful in a new, more competitive global economy will be more flexible, responsive, and leaner than those in the past. Products and services must be brought to market faster, quality must be improved, and information is needed as the connecting thread throughout the organization. We simply cannot wait for typed memos to make their way up through an organizational maze until they reach the one true leader. Small groups must tackle problems and seize opportunities as they arise. Individuals at all levels need the responsibility and authority to make decisions.

Where will companies find these Twenty-first-Century Leaders? They will recruit them from college campuses. Increasingly, the kinds of leadership skills you have acquired and can demonstrate will be critical to your career in business. This simply means that you must, from the day you walk through the gates at your college or university, look for courses, mentors, independent study projects, and extracurricular activities that will enhance your ability to lead. Seek them out, find them, and then work hard at developing your skills.

There are, as noted, many books and articles on this topic. In any bookstore you can find dozens. But we would like to leave you with a short list of guiding principles to get you started. Larry Ludewig, former dean of students at Texas Tech University, recently wrote an article entitled "The Ten Commandments of Effective Leadership." As effectively as any of the 300-page books we have seen, these ten commandments get to the core of what leadership is all about.

1. *Thou shalt know thyself and like what thou knowest.* You cannot be an effective leader without knowing your own strengths and weaknesses. Your self-assessment must be continuous and as objective as you can make it. Knowing your capabilities will allow you to improve on your weaknesses and trade on your strengths.

2. *Thou shalt not be what thou wishest not to lead.* Bozos tend to breed bozos. So if you do not relish the idea of leading a bunch of clowns, you'd better not be one yourself. If you expect no more from others than what you yourself are willing to give, and if you give to any project what you can legitimately give, you will never be disappointed in your leadership results.

3. *Thou shalt learn more and communicate better if thy ears are open and thy mouth is shut.* Most problems that leaders are asked to solve are people problems. Most people problems are created because of a failure in communication. Most failures in communication are the result of people hearing but not listening to one another.

4. *Thou shalt know thy team and be a team player.* As a leader, you must make the effort to know what other members of the team are doing, not necessarily to monitor their progress but to seek ways and means of providing your own assistance. Leaders look for opportunities to lend a hand.

5. *Thou shalt be honest to thyself as well as others.* All good leaders make mistakes, a host of them. Rarely, however, do they make the same

mistake more than once. And when they do err in deed or judgment, they openly admit their mistake, learn from it, and forget it. Generally, others will forget it too.

6. *Thou shalt not avoid risks; thou shalt manage them.* If you are to become an effective leader, you will need to become an effective risk taker. Generally being optimists, effective leaders see problems as challenges, challenges as catalysts for change, and changes as opportunities. They do not avoid failure; they seek success.

7. *Thou shalt believe in thyself before any others shall.* All effective leaders share one characteristic: confidence in their own ability to get the job done. This personal confidence is often contagious and quick to permeate an entire organization, boosting confidence levels of all team members (in themselves and in their leader).

8. *Thou shalt know that offense doth always outscore defense.* The most effective leaders are quicker to act than react. Their best solution to any problem is to solve it before it becomes a problem. They much prefer winning to whining. If they see something that needs fixing, they will do what they can to repair it before being told to do so by someone else.

9. *Thou shalt know the ways of disagreement and the means of compromise.* People disagree with one another. But keep in mind that you are not engaged in combat. The point is not who will win or lose, who will be the victor or the vanquished; the real winner is the leader who can facilitate the opposing side's goals while achieving his or her own.

10. *Thou shalt not lead before thou followest.* Rarely will an effective leader fail to be an effective follower. There are probably many reasons why this is true, but the most important is a corollary to the golden rule we learned, and largely ignored, as children: Effective leaders lead as they would like to be led.

Source: Larry Ludewig, "The Ten Commandments of Leadership," *NASPA* (National Association of Student Personnel Administrators) *Journal,* Spring 1988, p. 297. Reprinted with permission of *NASPA,* © 1988.

III
The Commitment

10

Taking It to
the Max

Let's take a moment for a short review. It's not so easy to acquire all the skills we've identified in previous chapters; it takes time, effort, and a real commitment to develop these talents. In fact, it is far easier to conclude that being a good problem solver is more important in business than figuring out *how* to become a good problem solver. In order to illustrate this point, we contrast two recent major research reports that say a lot about business careers and college graduates.

The findings of the first study are detailed in a book we have mentioned several times, Lyman Porter's and Lawrence McKibbin's *Management Education and Development: Drift or Thrust into the 21st Century?* (1988). As we noted, this study was conducted for the American Assembly of Collegiate Schools of Business, the major accrediting agency for business schools in the United States. The authors surveyed CEOs and personnel directors, business school deans and faculty members, plus business students and graduates from across the country, asking a broad range of questions. One question we want to focus on is "What are the major strengths of business school graduates?" Table 12 shows the percentage of corporate respondents who found a particular quality to be a "major strength" of business program graduates.

Our contrast point comes from a 1989 book by Boston University professor Michael Useem, *Liberal Education and Corporate America.* Useem's work was supported in part by the Corporate Council on the Liberal Arts, an organization that tries to promote a better understanding of the relationship between a (traditional) liberal arts education and effective management in the corporate world. Useem, unlike Porter and McKibbin, surveyed only corporate respondents, focusing on middle- and senior-level managers. Again, while Useem's study addressed a broad range of issues, we need to concentrate on

Table 12. Business Majors and Liberal Arts Graduates: A Study in Contrasts

Perceived Strengths of Business Graduates*   **Above-Average Qualities of Liberal Arts Graduates†**

Skill Area	Percent Checking "Major Strength"	Personal Qualities	Percent Stating Above Average
High motivation to work	38	Communication skills	85
Analytical skills	19	Understanding people	71
Knowledge of a particular content area	16	Appreciating ethical concerns	66
Appropriate self-confidence	16	Innovativeness	52
Oral communication	11	Leadership skills	51
Computer skills	9	Ability to analyze and prioritize	43
Leadership/interpersonal skills	7	Analytical skills	43
Realistic expectations	5	Understanding company environment	38
Maturity	5	Understanding company's internal world	38
Breadth of experience	5	Quantitative skills	20
Written communication skills	3	Disposition towards business	20
Knowledge of how the business world really operates	1	General business knowledge and skills	15
Understanding of legal/social/political environment	0	Technical knowledge and skills	7

*Porter and McKibbin   †Useem

one particular question: "On average, how would you assess liberal arts graduates on the following characteristics and skills?" The results of this question are also shown in Table 12. Look closely at the results of these two studies. What items cluster at the top of one list? What skills are at the bottom of the other? Taken together, these reports would seem to suggest that a business major is a liberal arts major turned upside down. For the most part, the strengths of the business students are the weaknesses of the liberal arts students, and vice versa.

- Liberal arts majors get high marks for communication skills; not so, business majors.

- Business majors are highly rated for their technical skills ("Knowledge of a particular content area"); liberal arts students do not rate well in this area.

- Leadership skills ranked fifth on Useem's list for liberal arts graduates and seventh on Porter's and McKibbin's list for business students. But look carefully at the numbers. Over half (51 percent) of Useem's respondents said that liberal arts graduates are above average in leadership skills. In contrast, just 7 percent of Porter's and McKibbin's respondents agreed that leadership skills are a perceived strength of business students.

Granted, these are not identical surveys with identical questions. But look carefully at these lists; do the analysis yourself. Put very simply, business schools produce people with excellent technical skills and poor people skills. In contrast, liberal arts graduates are perceived to have just the opposite qualities.

Interestingly, both these reports reached the same conclusion, even though they came at the problem from different directions. Listen to what Porter and McKibbin say at the conclusion of their book on business education.

> *On the basis of our interviews with senior managers in a variety of corporate and professional organizations, we believe any move by business schools toward broadening the academic experience of their students beyond the technical and functional will find enthusiastic endorsement by many employers.*

Perhaps not surprisingly, Useem offers a similar assessment in his book on the role of liberal arts education for future business professionals.

> *If management education should be broadened to include liberal learning, say many corporations, so too should liberal education be broadened to incorporate business learning. Indeed, the thrust of corporate preference would be for students in liberal arts and in management education to receive a healthy exposure to the other.*

The trick, it would seem, lies in your ability to see how things *interrelate*. For example, a student who wants to become a banker may see his or her future dependent upon technical proficiency. Given choices, this student would probably continue to take increasingly specialized courses in banking—capital budgeting, planning and control systems, mergers and acquisitions—to the exclusion of anything else. Technical expertise. Lots of it.

But the banking industry is looking for more than people who offer narrow specialization in banking and finance courses. Banks do not need one more faceless technocrat, one more number cruncher, one more blue suit. They need people who can create, change, communicate, and lead. The skills that the twenty-first-century banker needs exist in many different courses and many different books.

Clearly, the skills both large corporations and small businesses want do not reside in any single major or professional specialization. U.S. businesses need people with both practical skills and liberal

171

learning—both depth and breadth. Companies do not buy the myth that training for a professional career and getting a broad education in the humanities are mutually exclusive. Rather, today's smart businesses are greedy: They are on a talent hunt. They want students who can calculate a standard set of financial ratios *and* give a knockout presentation to a room full of senior executives. They want the employee who has *specific* skills in accounting procedures and also the *adaptive* skills of someone who knows how to learn, knows where to go for answers, and knows how to develop and communicate creative ideas. They need people who understand the fundamentals of computers but who also can be leaders.

Bankers' Reading List

If you were to compile a reading list of masterworks for bankers, works that would help them to be better managers of their employees, time, and businesses, which would you recommend?

Managers can learn more from the ancient Roman historian Fabius than from *Forbes,* says Professor John K. Clements, director of the Hartwick Humanities in Management Institute and professor of management at Hartwick College in Oneonta, N.Y. Clements suggests studying the following classics.

Homer, *The Iliad:* essential for bankers as team builders.

Machiavelli, *The Prince:* because that is the way it is; the uses and abuses of power.

Herman Melville, *Moby Dick:* the leader as cheerleader and motivator.

Arthur Miller, *Death of a Salesman:* because you cannot manage a sales force without it.

Plato, *The Republic* (selections): the best thing ever written on organizational design.

Plutarch, *Biography of Fabius: The Roman Consul:* decision making.

Plutarch, *Life of Alexander the Great:* acquisitions and mergers.

William Shakespeare, *King Lear:* succession planning and the importance of getting your employees to tell the truth.

Sophocles, *Antigone:* the importance of knowing when an organization needs to be told it is making a mistake and the value of women in management.

Henry David Thoreau, *On Walden Pond:* slimming down and restructuring a corporation.

Source: Roselyn Bernstein, *American Banker,* March 22, 1988, p. 24.

The moral of this story is that students of the 1990s who aspire to a business career need to extend themselves beyond the standard business course work.

The Campus Outside the Classroom

The extending we are referring to should not end with the course work described in Chapters 3 through 9. Choosing courses is still a gross simplification of what college offers. We have made it seem as though college revolves solely around classes. Indeed, we have spent seven chapters advising you on the specific classes that relate to your future in business. But college students spend only 10 to 15 percent of their time in class, maybe 20 hours a week at best out of a 168-hour week. What do you do with the rest of your time? Certainly a large part of your time goes to the necessities—sleeping, eating, and so on. You also spend some hours just hanging out with friends. We hope you spend at least 20 hours each week reading and studying.

Let's take a closer look at this issue. If you're like many college students, you may manage your money far better than you budget your time. But time is a very valuable resource.

Time management experts say that one way to learn about effective time management is to keep an accurate diary for a week: Record how you spend each hour of the day before you go to bed at night. Classes, studying in the library, an hour at the gym, personal reading, meals, doing volunteer work, talking with friends, performing lab experiments, shopping, part-time job—these things all take time.

Look at the basic week: seven days, 168 hours. Okay, the "fixed expenses," such as sleeping, getting dressed, and meals, probably account for over 9 hours a day, or 65 hours a week, or almost 40 percent of your week. Then add another 15 to 20 hours each week for classes and labs if you're a full-time student, plus 30 hours (or probably much more) for reading and studying. Two thirds of your week (115 of the 168 hours) are gone before you have that first extended conversation with a friend, spend an hour exercising in the gym or jogging, or work a single shift at your part-time job.

How *do* you use the remaining 53 hours? How *can* you make the best and most effective use of your remaining time? Part-time job? Conversations with faculty? Extra time studying? Volunteer work? Community service? Exercising? Partying? These activities reflect choices. Your responsibility is to manage your time as you manage your money. Both are limited resources. And time is exactly like money: You can never recover it if you've spent it foolishly.

Your waking hours not spent in classes present opportunities to prepare for your future. They may not involve structured learning situations (no professor, no grade book). But the experiences you have outside the college classroom can be just as useful as any lecture or homework assignment. In some cases, even more useful. Many college professors lecture to their students. They stand in front of a classroom and outline critical issues. They identify relevant examples and fill the chalkboard with formulas. Students dutifully copy everything in notebooks, which they study ferociously before each exam and then reproduce on quizzes and tests. Students do learn through this process, but this way of learning has its limitations. For one, it is passive: Students do little more than memorize—cram, if you will—and then regurgitate.

Carnation Company

Carnation Company is part of Nestlé's $20 billion multinational food and grocery products operation. It is headquartered in Los Angeles and has over 10,000 employees. Tony Burnham, Carnation's former vice president of human resources and management, worked closely with his campus recruiters to keep Carnation's corporate ranks full: "When I was at Carnation, we looked for the intangibles in our recruiting. It seemed as though everyone had a marketing or finance degree and a 3.0 GPA. But what separated them was that some people had a sense of purpose, a sense of themselves. When you asked them questions such as 'What's important to you?' or 'What are you particularly good at?' they were able to articulate ideas about themselves. These were the kinds of people we needed. Ones that looked to themselves for answers, who were spirited and entrepreneurial. They didn't expect the company to tell them what to do. They were self-sufficient.

"Perhaps the biggest problem that many corporations face is reactivity. So many students want to be molded; they want to be told what to do. They see a job as an extension of the classroom; the company defines the job to them and then they repeat it back, day in, day out, over the course of a career. It's like taking an exam every day. Well, corporations and small businesses aren't that interested in hiring those kinds of people. They look beyond a student's college, major, and GPA to try and identify a set of experiences that give someone a stronger sense of self. It's critical because you can't empower other people if you don't know yourself. And that's what it takes to manage today's successful company: individuals who can act responsibly on their own strengths and directions and hold themselves accountable."

A broader, less reactive view of learning is taken by Alexander Astin of UCLA, one of higher education's most respected scholars. Astin's approach is quite simple: *Students learn by becoming in-volved.* Involvement refers to the amount of physical and psychological energy that the student devotes to the academic experience. The importance of involvement has been confirmed in many studies of persistence (trying to understand the differences between students who enroll in college but never finish and those who persist and earn their degree).

In general, the things that facilitate persistence all signify high involvement: studying hard, living on campus, interacting frequently with other students and with faculty, and participation in extracurricular activities. These extracurricular (outside-the-classroom) activities do more than enhance your chances of graduating; they also are related to career development and success. One example: A massive, two-decade-long study of job performance and mobility among AT&T executives reveals that leadership experience—student government, the school newspaper, the debate team—was *a much better long-term predictor of managerial performance than were college grades*. Another study of corporation presidents showed that three out of four held at least one student office in a campus organization during their years in college.

Colleges and universities are loaded with opportunities that promote personal and professional growth. Internships, student exchange programs, athletics, student government, independent study projects, and professional organizations are all means for involvement. The thing these activities have in common is *experiential education,* or learning by doing: They engage or involve the student directly in a topic area and allow the student to apply the knowledge gained in the classroom. Perhaps the ancient Chinese proverb says it best: "I hear and I forget; I see and I remember; I do and I understand."

Of course, the first few weeks on a college campus are an unnerving experience for most students. Everything you've been accustomed to is irrelevant. Your life is turned topsy-turvy. All the old familiar faces are replaced by new ones: roommates, classmates, professors. No one tells you when to come home or what to wear or urges you to get your elbows off the table. You don't get home-cooked meals on a campus. Given these changes, it is understandable that you try to settle into a pattern or a standard set of daily activities. The problem arises when the pattern becomes a routine, extending to classes. Many students see courses as part of the routine: They go to class; they come back; when they finish a semester or term, they grab a catalog and select

© 1989 by Heiser Zedonek

another bunch of classes. It's like following a recipe in a cookbook or filling in the blanks. The adventure that a college education should be is reduced to a numbering exercise: Ten courses down, thirty to go.

It can be difficult to break out of the comfortable routine of courses, but a rewarding and successful college education includes the search for interesting and involving experiences that will help you develop, as Tony Burnham, former vice president of human resources and management at Carnation, puts it, "a stronger sense of self." So, it is essential that you explore the campus, seek out opportunities, and gather experiences.

Let's look at four learning-by-doing activities that are the most useful and important for acquiring business skills: internships, professional associations, part-time jobs, and team activities (sports and student government).

A Peek at the Real World

Internships offer experiences in which students learn by taking on responsible roles as workers in organizations. But we mean more than just working, just putting in the hours; internships provide an opportunity to observe and reflect on what happens in an organization. Internship opportunities exist in almost every kind of organization—nonprofit agencies, government offices, small businesses, and large corporations. Currently one of every five college students completes an internship experience as an undergraduate. This rate is seven times higher than it was ten years ago, according to the National Society for Internships and Experiential Education.

Companies realize that internships provide valuable real-world experience for students. Firms also recognize that internships yield hard evidence about job performance. They can use the internship evaluation in addition to other information—responses in an interview, recommendations, and academic record—*before* deciding whether to make a job offer. Sterling C. Gatling, a placement supervisor for Dow Chemical, suggests that internships are a rich source of information for potential employers: "You get to take a look at a future employee over a three-month period. You get information you can't possibly get from a college transcript." (Dow employed 368 students as interns during the summer of 1989.) Judy Palmer, an internship coordinator at Smith College, says that employers see internships as "a prerecruiting method." The St. Paul–based 3M Company, for example, now offers half its interns permanent positions after graduation.

From the student's perspective, too, an internship makes good sense. Here are four of the many benefits of an internship experience, cited by Timothy Stanton and Kamil Ali in their book *The Experienced Hand: A Student Manual for Making the Most of an Internship.*

1. *Employment.* With a tight economy and fewer jobs available, students with internship experience stand out in the job hunt. An internship can help you extricate yourself from the "can't get a job without experience, can't get experience without a job" double bind.

2. *Take charge of your learning.* Internships are important opportunities for you to design your own learning curriculum and get away from the campus-based one that may be frustrating you.

3. *Theory into practice.* An internship experience can add more meaning to academic study by giving you the chance to apply theories learned in class to real-life situations.

4. *Personal growth.* Having to solve problems in unfamiliar situations can bolster your self-confidence and show you where you need to work. It can be an important growth experience.

In a more scientific way, research has examined the individual effect of college internship experiences. An interesting set of research findings comes from Professor M. Susan Taylor of the University of Maryland. She compared two groups of college students: those who had completed an internship and those who had not. Her research indicated that internships lead to a "greater crystallization of vocational self-concept and of values regarding work-related outcomes." In other words, interns get a better handle on what they want to do and what they want from a job. Interns also experience greater employment opportunities, receive significantly higher starting salaries, and express greater satisfaction with the accepted job offer.

Business internship opportunities are fairly common. For example, a recent nationwide study reported in the *CPA Journal* indicates that more than two thirds of responding institutions offered internship programs in accounting. Most programs, according to the survey, have some type of academic requirement to determine eligible student candidates. Typical requirements include completion of a minimum number of credit hours, completion of specified accounting courses, and possession of a minimum grade point average. Perhaps the most significant finding was that at the conclusion of the internship period over 75 percent of student interns received and accepted an offer of permanent employment from the firm at which they had interned.

Cooperative education programs offer a different kind of internship opportunity. Students in co-op programs usually alternate semesters on campus and semesters at work. Unlike the accounting internship cited above, internships are a mandatory component of co-op programs. Over 1,000 two-year and four-year colleges now offer co-op degree programs, in partnership with some 50,000 employers. For example, the University of Cincinnati has over 4,000 co-op students employed in 1,200 organizations in thirty-five states.

Finally, there are international programs. Some colleges and universities have internship and co-op agreements with companies in foreign countries. The International Association of Students in Economics and Business Management (AIESEC), a forty-two-year-old student-run organization, gives students the opportunity to complement their education with practical business exposure in any of seventy participating countries, including the USSR. According to AIESEC, members "gain valuable experience and training on several levels: through the extensive international traineeship exchange program, which involves over 6,000 AIESEC members yearly; and the experience of managing the local chapters of AIESEC, which are run as businesses."

Internship Readiness Quiz:
A Questionnaire for Students

Are You Ready for an Internship?

At what point in a student's course of study is it advisable to pursue an internship? The Internship Readiness Quiz has been designed specifically to answer this question. By taking this quiz you are making the first step in planning your internship. This is a self-scoring instrument. After answering the questions, add up your score to determine whether you can make all of the provisions necessary for tackling an internship. . . . Good luck!

Answer all questions to the best of your knowledge. Rate each statement using the following scale: Strongly agree = 5; Agree = 4; Uncertain = 3; Disagree = 2; Strongly disagree = 1.

Score

_____ 1) It is difficult to find summer employment relating to my academic and career goals.

_____ 2) I sometimes wonder how what I have been learning [in school] applies to the world of work.

_____ 3) I have taken courses relevant to my career interests, or I plan to next semester.

_____ 4) As I observe other students who seemingly have more extensive work experience, I wish there was some way to get experience related to my future career plans.

_____ 5) It would be possible to adjust my courses for next semester so that I would have at least ten hours of open time per week to work at an internship off campus.

_____ 6) It would not be necessary for me to earn a salary if I were to consider an internship.

_____ 7) I really have no idea whether or not I will attend graduate school, because I don't have the foggiest notion what I would study.

_____ 8) I am experiencing some boredom with my classes and want to pursue other extracurricular activities.

_____ 9) My parents ask me, "What are you going to do after you graduate from [college]?" And I don't know.

_____ 10) This coming summer, I would consider working part-time and interning part-time without pay.

Scale:

Definitely ready for an internship 45–50
Ready for an internship 40–44
Need to consider potential obstacles
  before starting an internship 35–39
It will take careful planning and rethinking of
  priorities if you want to begin an internship 30–34
It may be in your best interest to consider
  other options . . . . under 30

Source: An exhibit, by Michael Soler, reprinted from *Experiential Education Newsletter,* January–February 1989. National Society for Internships and Experiential Education, 3509 Hayworth Street, Suite 207, Raleigh, NC 27609.

In general, internships are an ideal way to extend yourself beyond the classroom. Internships are *involving* experiences. Think of an internship as part of your professional training, much like the medical residency experience, the student teaching experience, and the architect's apprenticeship experience. Shouldn't you, with a future in business, attempt to get some practice before you join the real world beyond the campus walls?

Joining Professional Associations and Clubs

Most college libraries have a reference book called the *Encyclopedia of Associations*. This is a large book. It fills three separate volumes and includes large associations (for example, the 300,000-member AFL-CIO) as well as small associations that have no more than a P.O. box and an annual newsletter. It is hard to imagine an industry or field that does not have at least one professional association. Most have several, and some have upwards of a dozen.

Many professional associations sponsor student chapters on college campuses. The American Advertising Federation (AAF), for example, is a national organization of over 200 ad clubs (each including large and small advertising agencies, advertisers, media groups, and advertising-related services) and 35,000 individual members. The AAF also has a college chapter program that includes 135 colleges and universities representing over 4,000 advertising students. Each local chapter elects its own officers, admits and initiates student members, plans campus activities (including discussion groups and seminars with professionals), and promotes visits to advertisers, agencies, media, and nearby AAF ad clubs. Since 1975 the AAF has also sponsored the National Student Advertising Competition, in which student teams must solve a real advertising problem presented by a real corporate client; entries are judged by the sponsoring client. College chapters are provided with a case study outlining the history of the client's product and current advertising situation. The case studies are candid and reflect a real situation. The students research the product and its competition, identify potential problem areas, and devise a complete advertising/marketing campaign for the client. In 1986 Iowa State University won the national competition; the client was Levi Strauss & Company. In 1987 Brigham Young University walked off with top honors for its Chevrolet campaign. The University of Oregon won the 1988 competition sponsored by Nestlé Enterprises. And in 1989 a new champion emerged.

And the Winner Is . . .

Before a standing-room-only crowd at the AAF National Advertising Conference in Washington, D.C., the University of West Florida, Pensacola, was proclaimed winner of the 1989 National Student Advertising Competition. The daylong competition of fifteen student-team finalists competing for top honors, culled from 122 college and university teams that participated in fifteen regional semifinal competitions, was judged by a tough five-person panel from the client company—Kellogg Company of Battle Creek, Michigan—and its advertising agency.

The 1989 competitors were required to develop a name, packaging, pricing, marketing strategy, media plan, and advertising campaign for a wheat cereal that Kellogg had developed as a potential new product. UWF's winners dubbed the cereal Basics, aiming their campaign at baby boomers, especially women, considered new traditionalists. The campaign was built around the slogan "Outwardly simple, inwardly rich."

According to UWF's faculty adviser, Professor Tom Groth, the effort was a "heroic" one: "We spent almost a full year on the project. There were long hours and a lot of frustration involved, but I think all of the students would say that it was worth it. The hands-on, out-of-classroom challenges will give these students the edge. They can think on their feet, they became 'street smart,' and they learned a lot of important lessons that would have been impossible to teach in a regular course."

Pat Holcombe, a UWF team member, used the experience to help get his current position as advertising production assistant at the *Atlanta Constitution:* "They looked at the school and my degree, but what made the difference was my extracurricular activities. It definitely gave me an edge. They knew that I had already been in deadline situations and had made sacrifices. I had helped produce a winner, and that meant more to them than my GPA or whether I had taken all my accounting classes. I didn't have to talk about what I could do; I showed them what I had done."

Need other examples of professional associations' interest in college students? The Operations Research Society of America (ORSA) and The Institute of Management Sciences (TIMS) work closely with college campuses having OR or MS programs (involving the application of scientific principles to assist management decision making). Operations research problems, for example, involve finding the shortest or quickest route from one location to another or deciding when and where a company should distribute a new product and at what price. ORSA/TIMS jointly publish *OR/MS Today,* a professional journal for all their members. They send *Student Communications,* a newsletter that details research opportunities, conferences, and paper competitions and has a special emphasis on the "transition from student to member of industry," to student associate members of ORSA. Finally, they produce a detailed brochure, *Careers in Operations Research,* that identifies educational programs in operations research and describes typical careers in OR, using recent college graduates as examples.

The American Marketing Association (AMA) has an international network of 100 professional chapters, with almost 30,000 members, and 350 collegiate chapters, serving some 20,000 student members. Students and collegiate chapters are entitled to an extensive list of benefits.

- *Marketing News* keeps students up-to-date on their profession and provides them with information on careers and AMA activities.

- *Regional collegiate conferences* feature research sessions on different marketing fields.

- *Computerized student job bank* enables employers and imminent graduates to request lists of potential employees and employers, by the specific areas of location, field, salary, and so on.

- *Marketing strategy competition* is designed to test the marketing skills of AMA collegiate members by asking them to develop a marketing strategy for a national nonprofit organization.

- *AMA speakers list* is a complete list of professional speakers, including presentation ratings, fees (if any), and topics they will discuss.

- *Careers in Marketing* is a booklet designed to inform students about different marketing careers.

- *The Employment Kit* is a booklet designed to inform students of the necessary skills required for the career search, including resumes and cover and thank-you letters.

Obviously, a joiner has a number of advantages. A professional association—AAF, ORSA/TIMS, AMA, or any other—is a professional network. Student members can talk to people who are practicing the profession. These people are usually more than willing to share their experiences; they are often on the lookout for talent for their firms! Regional meetings may be informal monthly opportunities to listen to knowledgeable speakers, learn more about the field, and meet working professionals. The network is a source of local, regional, and national contacts that can be very useful during your job search, both for summer work and for a permanent position after graduation. Belonging to a professional association can also help you sharpen your focus. The desire simply to be a manager is not specific enough, and any general field, say, accountancy, is also too broad. You need to know the type of industry in which you want to pursue a management career and your area of special interest (cost accounting, public accounting, and so on).

Joining a professional association can also provide you with some practical accomplishments; for example, serving as a chapter officer and working on a project like the AAF's competition are deeds, not just words. And such deeds can raise one student out of the undifferentiated mass of thousands—no, hundreds of thousands—of business majors graduating each year.

Working Part-Time

The world of a working college student can easily be divided into two parts: on campus and off campus. Many colleges and universities rely heavily on students to staff offices and operations. Students now work in virtually every area of a college, answering phones in department offices, performing secretarial duties, working in the library, driving shuttle buses, taking visitors on tours, acting as assistants in chemistry labs, selling books in the campus store. Many students have work-study jobs, generally on-campus employment supported in part by federal funds as a form of student financial aid. The other option, of course, is to work in local businesses, restaurants, hotels, gas stations, and so forth.

According to a recent survey commissioned by the Carnegie Foundation for the Advancement of Teaching, almost two thirds of today's undergraduates work while they are in college; 40 percent have part-time jobs and 23 percent work full-time. Does working help or hurt your studies? Does it have an effect on your life—helping you earn money to cover the costs of going to college or perhaps giving you a little more spending money?

In general, research shows that students who work at part-time jobs on campus (15–20 hours or less per week) generally earn better grades and are more likely to graduate than are their peers who either do not work or work at full-time jobs. Why? First, students with multiple demands on their time are forced to become better organized. Working students are also often more highly motivated than nonworking students. Finally, they gain self-confidence and acquire a sense of purpose, and these have positive effects on academic work. Results of a study reported in the *Economics of Education Review* suggest that "college students' in-school work experience appears to have a significant positive effect on their post-college earnings for at least five years."

A 1990s student might do well to supplement course work with a part-time, on-campus job—*but not just any job.* There are usually enough opportunities on campus for you to choose one that relates to your career interest or one that can help you explore potential career alternatives. For example, an advertising major might look for work in the public relations office. An accounting major might look for part-time work in a department's business office or in the campus accounting office.

Soccer, Saxophones, and Student Government

From early morning until late into the night, life on a college campus involves a stream of activities. In addition to the mass of students going back and forth to classes, there are also bands practicing, clubs meeting, and staff members rushing to meet a newspaper deadline. Extracurricular activities provide great ways to build on the skills discussed in this book.

- *Student government:* The Twenty-first-Century Leader gets to practice the fine arts of negotiation and persuasion.

- *Campus newspaper:* Our Great Communicator is alive and well, polishing prose for columns and stories.

- *Debate team:* The Problem Solver develops and evaluates arguments in competitions.

- *Advisory boards:* The Change Maker provides creative input to the deliberations of campus committees and in conversations with academic leaders.

- *Athletics:* The Team Player is essential to success in any team sport.

- *Volunteer activities:* A volunteer gets to exercise communication, leadership, technological, problem-solving, change-making, and team-player skills.

These activities provide rich experiences that last well beyond graduation day. Lessons learned on the athletic field or as an officer in a student organization will permanently change your view of the world. Not too long ago, several organizational researchers conducted a comprehensive analysis of factors that influenced the careers of CEOs of the nation's 800 largest industrial corporations and service firms.

One of their more interesting findings (published in *CEO: Who Gets to the TOP in America?*) was that "chief executive[s] are at least 12 times as likely as today's typical college student to have participated in intercollegiate athletics." Approximately one third of all CEOs participated in at least one intercollegiate sport—compared with only 2 percent of college students doing so!

Some examples: IBM CEO John Akers was a hockey player at Yale; C. J. Silas, CEO at Phillips Petroleum Company, earned a varsity letter in basketball at Georgia Tech; CEOs David Packard (Hewlett-Packard), Donald Rumsfeld (formerly of G. D. Searle, a large pharmaceutical company), and Paul Choquette (Gilbane Building Company, construction) were varsity football players. Alex Kroll, CEO of Young & Rubicam (advertising) was an all-American center on Rutgers' football team.

Many of the CEOs in the study reported that playing sports helped them learn teamwork and interpersonal skills, qualities that were useful after graduation. Six-foot-six C. J. Silas of Phillips Petroleum says it well:

> *You realize quickly that you can't do it all yourself. If one man is a better shot than the other, they feed him the ball. You play the game around the team you have, just as you adjust to skills in management.*

James Moffett is another good example. Today he is the CEO of Freeport-McMoran, Inc., a New Orleans–based natural resources firm; as a college student years ago he played varsity football for the University of Texas. Moffett remembers that his coaches selected a first team each and every day.

> *They did that to remind the players that they could change the lineup if a player didn't produce. You were never sure you made the first team until you went into that locker room and walked up to that list to see your name. It reminded you that you had to work hard every day, that your performance wasn't based on what you did last year or last week, but what you are doing now.*

That lesson stuck with Moffett, and it is not a bad one for a business leader of the twenty-first century to have learned in college—*even if it wasn't in a classroom.*

The Life and Times of a Minimalist

"Suppose," said the professor to the incoming freshmen, "that by paying a modest sum, you could get a permit to go into the largest store and help yourself to everything—diamonds, precious stones, watches, sporting goods, expensive clothing—the only limit being what you could carry away. Only a fool would say, 'Guess I'll take a pair of socks and some golf balls.'"

Yet consider the logic of the student who pays for a college education that entitles him or her to absorb, to the limit of his or her capacity, the accumulated wisdom of the ages, to gain intimate acquaintance with the geniuses in many disciplines, and to acquire knowledge of the universe, our planet, our social and economic systems and who then says, "Guess I'll find an easy major, avoid the tough classes and professors, and do just enough to get by."

Let's be honest. Every college or university has an unwritten but understood acceptable minimum. You can choose an easy major and get a straight C average. You can search for the "gut" courses—embarrassingly easy ones, either because the work is a breeze or simply because there isn't much work in them. You can schedule all your classes for after 10 a.m. because you like to party at night and then sleep late. You can find the geography professor who gives the same exams year in, year out, the semiretired psychology professor who awards everyone a B, or perhaps a class called Beginning Volleyball or Understanding Yourself. You can avoid getting involved. Unfortunately, thousands of students approach a college education this way. Just get a degree. Don't raise a sweat.

Just getting a business degree is not the answer. You simply cannot allow yourself to think that sixteen courses in business are all you need to prepare for a lifetime of learning and earning. That's terribly shortsighted. Getting an undergraduate degree, whatever the major, is not one-stop shopping; everything needed for success is not laid out for quick and effortless consumption. Minimal effort in any area, whether business or biology, will reap a minimal reward. No pain, no gain.

Now is the time to invest in your future. Your investment must be as broad and as dynamic as possible. Run for student government, join the band, play a sport, get to know a professor or two on a personal level. *Just do it.* Register for an internship, join a club, become a member of a professional organization. Get a part-time job. Take advantage of the wonderful opportunities that a college campus offers. Get involved up to your neck. Be aggressive; go after the things that you want out of a college education, both inside and outside the classroom. Don't be a minimalist. Do the most you can do—*do the max.*

11

Seven Little Lighthouses

We wrote this book to be a guide, to help you chart your way through the unfamiliar territory from campus to career. But unlike the authors of most travel guides, we have not attempted to help you choose a destination. Instead, our efforts have focused on making the journey itself significantly more rewarding by helping you *add value* to your college degree.

We have tried to assist your journey in two ways. First, we have given you a series of signposts. These markers provide some idea of what lies ahead; that is, they suggest the skills you will need to compete successfully in the business world. The journey is not unlike that of a ship slicing through the darkness of a foggy night. According to one story, a navy ship was cruising along when a sudden blip appeared on its radar screen. The unknown object was straight in front of the ship, threatening a head-on collision. The communication between the ship and unknown object went as follows.

From the bridge of the navy vessel:
"Alter your course 10 degrees North."

The reply (coming back out of the fog):
"Alter your course 10 degrees South."

The bridge sends out a second message:
"Alter your course 10 degrees North. I am a captain in command."

The reply:
"Alter your course 10 degrees South. I am a seaman second class."

The third message goes out from the navy ship:
"I order you to change immediately. We are a battleship."

And the reply:
"I suggest you may wish to change your course very soon. We are a lighthouse."

We have tried to alert you to the rocky shoals and shallow waters of using your college experience to prepare for a business career. We have tried to highlight the differences between a traditional *business education* and an *education for a business career.* The traditional business education emphasizes accounting, marketing, finance, management, and other subject area issues. An education for a business career includes many of these subject area skills, but it also takes a much broader look at the business world and emphasizes the skills that will serve you well in a rapidly changing business environment.

This brings us to the second point: This knowledge or information is useful only if you choose to use it. We wrote this book to empower students, to give them the kind of information that often escapes even the most well-intentioned adviser. You should seek advice from professors, parents, and friends, but know that it is even more critical that *you* be informed. After all, this is your life; you make the choices, and you live with the outcomes. Our goal has been to provide some of that information, the signals that can help you negotiate treacherous waters; however, you must be the captain of your own ship. You cannot entrust these critical decisions to someone else. Your success in life—in professional activities and in your personal affairs—depends on *your* skills, *your* initiative, *your* sensitivity to the world and the people around you, and *your* decisions.

In this final chapter we offer seven additional tips for students planning a career in business. You might think of these as seven additional lighthouses for the beginning sailor.

1. Package Yourself Creatively

One of the first concepts you learn in a marketing course is "product differentiation." *What is product differentiation?* A perfect example of product differentiation is the Sony Walkman, a very familiar product to most college students. The initial success of the Walkman when it was introduced in 1983 was not based upon advertising, price, or promotional sales. Instead, its success was driven by the simple notion that it was distinctive. It was special. There were ample radios and tape cassette players, in all sizes, shapes, and colors, on the market, but all shared a similar feature: They had speakers for the world to hear. Sony's product was a portable concert that played for one person. You could listen to whatever you wanted, wherever you wanted, and play it as loud as your eardrums could stand. It provided product differentiation because it offered the customer a *unique feature.* The Sony Walkman was one of the most successful (and subsequently most imitated) new products of the 1980s.

We would like for you to begin to think of yourself as one of the most successful "new products" of the 1990s. You don't come off the end of a production line, and you are not mass marketed on television; yet you do have a series of personal attributes that are not unlike those of a manufactured product. A Walkman has a certain look, and so do you. The Walkman can perform a series of tasks, and you have a set of skills. As Sony advertises the Walkman's distinctive features, at some point during college you will put together a resume to promote yourself to potential employers, and you'll want to emphasize your distinctive features. Why should a recruiter invite *you* in for an interview? Why should a large corporation or a small business hire *you?* What do *you* offer a future employer that is potentially distinctive or unique? What do *you* have to contribute that will help the firm function more effectively, gain greater market share, design better products, enhance service, make better use of marketing information, or successfully resolve any of the hundreds of large and small challenges that confront a business on any given day?

And one more thing: As we noted in the first chapter of this book, you will be facing competition. In fact, your competition is stiffer than the competition Sony confronted when it launched the Walkman. Sony had no more than thirty or forty competitors. As a college graduate seeking your first job, you will be competing against over a million other college students. If you're a business major, you're part of a very large club; 250,000 students earn undergraduate business degrees each year. *So what makes you distinctive?*

One thing that we suggest is to offer the customer—in this case, your potential employer—some creative packaging. The best way to do this is to think in terms of a combining strategy unlikely to be seen in other job applicants. Here are a few examples, drawn from the real-life experiences of some of our former students.

- One young woman transferred to the University of Rhode Island from another school, where she had been a chemistry major. Although she had taken only three chemistry courses, she realized that she didn't want to spend her life in a lab. In fact, she began to think that her real skills might be in sales. After completing several marketing courses, she decided to change her major to business; however, she continued to take a chemistry course every term. Two years later she graduated with a business degree in marketing. Unlike any of her classmates, however, she also graduated with a minor in chemistry. Four major drug companies offered her a job in pharmaceutical sales.

- The College of William and Mary in Virginia has a fairly quantitative business program that requires lots of statistics, economics, and computer courses. One William and Mary student who was interested in advertising thought that a "business" major was her only choice. After doing poorly in the quantitative courses, she began to look for another way to "package" herself. She talked to advertising people and then shifted into psychology. Why psychology? Because advertising is primarily applied psychology. She also took a minor in marketing (to learn more about business), loaded up on English courses (to help improve her writing skills), and did an internship in her senior year with a local advertising agency (to get some real-world experience). Today this student is happily employed in a Washington, D.C., ad agency.

- At Pepperdine University in California, a student we know faced the problem of *vocation* versus *avocation*. His avocation was art, but everyone, including his father, who was paying the tuition, impressed upon him the difficulty of succeeding as an artist. However, he was also pretty good with numbers and did quite well in a few introductory math courses. After a lot of reading and talks with people in different careers, he decided to pursue a career in art—but not as an artist. By majoring in accounting and minoring in art, he positioned himself as buyer for a major art gallery.

These examples show the wisdom of seeing yourself as a package—a series of attributes that *you can control*. The pharmaceutical companies, undoubtedly, interviewed a number of marketing majors. But how many of those applicants could understand the basic chemical compounds of their products? In turn, how many chemistry majors understand marketing and sales techniques? If you were the recruiter, whom would you choose—the chemistry major or the marketing major? How about the *one person* who knew both ends of the business? The other two students did the same thing: They put together a package—themselves—that was distinctive, that was different.

2. Develop a Personal Philosophy

Have you heard of Ivan Boesky? Known on Wall Street as "Ivan the Terrible," Boesky began serving a three-year prison term for insider trading in 1988. Before achieving this notoriety, at a commencement address at the University of California at Berkeley he observed that "greed is all right. . . . I want you to know that. I think greed is healthy. You can be greedy and feel good about yourself." The assembled graduates, ready for their new positions in the corporate world, cheered Boesky, applauding and laughing at the same time.

Do you remember the 1988 movie *Wall Street?* Michael Douglas, playing the lead role of Gordon Gekko, said, "Greed, for want of a better word, is good." *Is it?* We certainly saw a lot of greed in the past decade. The 1980s saw the defense industry under scrutiny for a long list of overcharges on government contracts, a multibillion-dollar savings and loan scandal, and widespread corporate pollution. "Being good" seems to have been replaced by "feeling good."

What is our hope for the future? Other morality indicators like crime and drug abuse rates all tell a sad story about the changing value systems in this country. And it is not all that comforting to know that almost 40 percent of college freshmen, and a higher percentage of business majors, admit to having cheated on tests in high school.

The emphasis in this book has been on acquiring skills during college to help you in your business career. Specifically, we have focused on those skills that can be learned in a classroom or through some other formal activity. But other factors are also very important; these other factors are not skills but, rather, personal qualities. A recent Michigan State University survey of some 800 businesses that employ new college graduates found that campus recruiters want more than team players who have well-developed leadership, problem-solving, and communication skills—skills that we have emphasized in this book. Also on the recruiters' skills list is a whole set of individual qualities: dependability, perseverance, reliability, honesty and integrity, maturity, and a sense of humor.

Certainly your major, grades, and college are important factors in the distinctive package you present to potential employers. However, you must remember that the firm, whether it's a major corporation or a small business, wants to hire a person, not a set of credentials. It needs people who have, as Tony Burnham put it, a "strong sense of self." So don't be surprised if a corporate recruiter begins an interview by asking, "What's important to you?" Recruiters know that good companies are not described in technical terms but in human terms. Good companies have megadoses of commitment, quality, spirit, and vision. You get that by staffing your organization with people who have developed a personal philosophy, people who *know* what's important to them and how it affects the world around them.

A growing number of colleges and universities in the United States offer courses in business ethics; some colleges require all business majors to take at least one business ethics course. Consider business ethics classes; do not dismiss them as a waste of your time. However, don't fool yourself into thinking that a few hours in a classroom *talking* about corporate and personal ethics will do the job. Your personal philosophy will emerge from real-life situations, especially those situations that force you to choose between two different value-laden alternatives. Throughout your college years, you will be exposed to people who hold radically different beliefs. Don't shy away from confronting such people or from facing tough issues in the classroom. Immerse yourself in moral dilemmas; wrestle with them. The purpose of education is to unsettle the mind, to widen horizons, to inflame the intellect. From controversy and uncertainty come wisdom, growth, and a set of values. For as a person is, so does that person act.

3. Take Charge

Some students go to college to learn; most go to be taught. There is a *huge* difference. *Being taught* implies passivity, restraint. In contrast, *learn* is an active verb that requires involvement, striving, choice, and participation. Students who go to college to be taught will be trampled by those who go to learn.

Virtually every college in the country assigns students to an adviser, sometimes a faculty member, sometimes a specialist whose job is exclusively academic advising. Most institutions require that your adviser review and approve your class list or registration papers. With your adviser's signature attached, you are allowed to sign up for courses on registration day. The rule of thumb, based upon our experience, is that the better students check with their adviser during the semester, ask questions, and review their options. They are squared away several weeks prior to the posted deadline. Average students show up on the day of registration and shove the form under an adviser's nose, asking, "Could you sign this for me?" The first group of students is proactive; the second, reactive.

Let's continue with this example. How does reactivity, or passivity, end up hurting the student? Classes at many colleges and universities, especially the ones taught by exceptional professors, are often oversubscribed. Demand exceeds supply. Consequently, more people want to be in the class than the professor is willing to have (or the classroom can accommodate). The striving student knows this and talks to the professor the semester before he or she plans to register for the class, expresses interest in the subject, asks for a course outline, and perhaps inquires about reading that might be done in advance. On the day of the first class, our striving student and the passive one may both be without chairs, on the waiting list. When the professor meets with "extras" after class and wants to know why they would like the class, the striver reminds the professor of their earlier meeting and the interest expressed at that time, whereas the other student usually announces, "I need a business class." One student is saying, "I am here to learn"; the other is saying, "Teach me something." The casual attitude of the latter always suggests someone reading off a shopping list: "Well, I need some potato chips, some bean dip, a six-pack of Coke, and a business class." Who do you think gets into the class?

This passive, or reactive, approach to your college experience will kill you. You may have heard that where you sit in a classroom determines your grade. It's true! Passive students tend to head for the back row, a safe place to hide from the instructor—or so they think! They are easily distracted, often daydream, and may even catch a few minutes of sleep from their perch at the back of the class. These are also the sudents who never join a business club, never become friends with a professor, never attempt an internship. And then they cannot understand their job-hunting problems when they graduate with no work experience, no references, no contacts, no extracurricular activities, and a solid C average.

You must understand that going to college is *your* job for the next few years. It is what you do. And no one at the school has been designated your fairy godmother; no one will be there to watch over and protect you. College faculty—and especially the best professors in all departments, who often have outside projects—are not going to spend their time tracking you down. Your adviser is not going to call your room to find out how your class schedule is going. The registrar's office is not about to harass you into making up a statistics class so that you can graduate on time.

We do!

This is your life, your career. And the choices are yours. The responsibility for them all rests with you—and you alone. Get in there, show some spirit, and take charge.

4. Understand Today's Career Options

There is an interesting story about Thomas Huxley, the nineteenth-century British biologist. One day Huxley was late in setting off to give a lecture. He jumped into a cab, crying, "Top speed!" The cabman whipped up his horse, and they set off as fast as the horse could go. A thought then dawned on Huxley; sticking his head out of the window, he called to the cabman, "Hey, do you know where I want to go?"

"No, your honor," shouted back the cabman, "but I'm driving as fast as I can."

As we pointed out in the first chapter, this book has little to say about your destination, where you want to go. From page 1, we have been like the cabman, setting off at top speed. Recognizing this, we would be remiss not to ask, *How important is destination?* In the world of careers, everyone is given the impression that a specific goal is very important. From the time a small child can speak, friends, relatives, and passersby repeat the same question: "What do you want to be when you grow up?" Under no circumstances is our little one allowed to voice any doubts or be noncommittal. The appropriate response is stated with firm conviction: "I want to be a doctor." Indeed, it is the proud parent who announces to all that third-grader Johnny has decided to become an astronaut or an accountant.

We suggest that you not commit yourself to investment banking and a degree in finance on the day after you arrive for freshman orientation. There are two good reasons. First, while fixing a destination may reduce anxiety and make everyone think that you are more mature and focused, the fact is that such clairvoyance is both a bit heroic and premature. The U.S. Department of Labor's massive *Occupational Outlook Handbook,* for example, lists 1,750 job categories. More are added to this list each year. So your task while in college is to eliminate 1,749 jobs from any further consideration. Good luck!

A second reason to avoid premature career commitments is that every futurist and career researcher sees more and more people experiencing—and enjoying—multiple careers. These multiple careers are also frequently unanticipated careers. The nice, neat, and very safe twenty- or thirty-year career path in a Fortune 500 company either doesn't exist anymore or is not as popular among employees as it once was. Upwards of half the people who begin their careers as just-out-of-college hires and management trainees at many large corporations leave these firms at the end of five years.

Some of today's hottest technology firms actually encourage their employees to look at their job experience in these tech shops as relatively short term, perhaps no more than a three- to five-year "tour of duty." Consider, for a moment, what Apple chairman and CEO John Sculley says about the people who come to work at Apple. "Many people [who come to companies like Apple Computer] aren't looking, after all, for [job] security. They're looking for personal growth, for a chance to make an important contribution. . . . People tend to look at joining a company like Apple as getting a graduate degree at a university. You select Apple because you think it can offer you an incredible, life-growing experience. . . . People gravitate to us with the idea of staying three to five years and then going off to start their own companies. And there can be no better preparation for it."

So, on the one hand, you are living in a world of transition, but on the other, you don't have years of time in college to spend exploring.

You need to pursue your options quickly and efficiently. Here are a few hints. First, visit your college or university's career planning and placement center. These offices typically offer a rich array of career-oriented workshops or courses. A career development course usually contains sections on (1) increasing knowledge about self (your aptitudes), (2) educational and occupational opportunities, and (3) job search skills. Second, do a little exploring on your own, reading books talking to people. There are a number of career development books available in both your college and local bookstores. For example, *Peterson's Job Opportunities for Business and Liberal Arts Graduates* is one of two annual directories of employment opportunities put out by the publisher of this book. Many business schools also have mentoring programs. If you want to know what an industrial statistician actually does, the school will schedule an informational interview with a graduate who is currently working in the field.

As we've noted, the most common question on a college campus may be "What's your major?" We are here to tell you that it is not a criminal offense to tell people that you are undeclared. A little uncertainty is okay. After all, Galileo studied medicine before turning to astronomy, George Washington was a land surveyor, Winston Churchill worked as a war correspondent, Ralph Waldo Emerson began his career as a clergyman, Albert Einstein was a mediocre patent examiner, and Virginia Graham was simply "the publisher's wife" before her husband's death led her to assume control of the *Washington Post*. Do these examples seem too historical, too remote? All right, then, let's look at some more recent examples from the 1980s.

- Mitch Kapor, founder of Lotus Development Corporation (as in Lotus 1-2-3), taught transcendental meditation and worked as a rock-and-roll disc jockey early in his career.

- Deborah Coleman, vice president for manufacturing at Apple Computer, Inc., and one of the most senior women in the computer industry, majored in anthropology as an undergraduate.

- Joseph Dionne, chairman and president of McGraw-Hill, Inc., was a high school teacher early in his career.

- Sherry Lansing was the first woman to head a major Hollywood studio. Did she rise to the top by beginning her management career in the studio mailroom? No! She had worked as a teacher and a model before she entered the entertainment business.

- Bill Campbell was once a football coach at Columbia University. He left coaching for a position at J. Walter Thompson, one of the nation's largest advertising agencies. He then took a job at

Kodak, later moved to Apple, and is now president of Claris, one of the nation's largest software companies.

- New York senator Daniel Patrick Moynihan worked on the docks in New York Harbor before going to college; he subsequently became a sociologist at Harvard and later held a series of diplomatic appointments before winning his first U.S. Senate race more than a decade ago.

In short, it is all right to be uncertain about your career, to explore different options while you are in college. However, what is not acceptable is being passive about the search. Applying the thinking that we suggested in the previous section, Take Charge, you should actively pursue your inclinations early. Try things, evaluate them, and then proceed accordingly. By understanding what career path you want to begin and then pursue, and *why* you want to pursue this career, you will be better able to choose your courses and other activities and to build a resume.

We are asking you to be a visionary and, further, to translate your visions into a series of decisions during your college career. Dream it— *then do it.*

5. Build a Resume

An artist going on a job interview takes along a portfolio of his or her work. During the interview the artist shows this work as prime examples of his or her skills, personal approach, and potential. The interviewer explains the specific commission and points to examples in the artist's portfolio that would apply to the job under discussion.

In the creative packaging section we talked about product differentiation to distinguish yourself from the hordes of graduates who will be sipping champagne on Commencement Day. An even more basic term that is important to you is *marketing,* especially as it relates to selling. Most people do not distinguish between marketing and selling, but a marketer knows that there is a tremendous difference.

Selling is the act of creating an exchange. I produce something, say, a widget, and then try to find someone who will buy it; there is an exchange of widgets for dollars. *Marketing,* in contrast, involves *satisfying need* and *creating demand* for a product or resource. First, I attempt to find out what the customer needs, and then I produce an item that has those need-satisfying features. Obviously selling is a part of marketing: Sales are made after time has been spent in listening to the consumer and then creating an appropriate product or service. It should be equally obvious that selling is a lot easier if you have a marketing orientation. The success of the Sony Walkman is a good example. The selling part was easy because a great deal of time and effort went into creating the *right* product: talking to consumers, trying various prototypes, satisfying a need.

A resume is a selling tool. It says to a prospective employer, "This is who I am." But more often than not, a graduate has given no thought to what an employer—the customer or "buyer" for new employees—really needs. There is a great difference between a resume that says, "This is who I am," and one that says, "This is what I can do for you." It is the difference between selling and marketing.

The best way to market yourself is to begin to think in terms of building a resume. And the best way to build a resume—or develop a marketing plan for anything that is for sale—is to listen to the customer. The first step is given in the title of the previous section—Understand Today's Career Options. Let's say that you are interested in becoming a certified public accountant (CPA). You should take an introduction to accounting course as soon as possible. You should also talk to your professors, join the Accounting Club, scan the *Journal of Accountancy,* and meet with a recent accounting graduate. Do everything you can to get a "feel" for the career and the course work. If it feels good, take a few more courses and ask some more questions. And don't be afraid to ask direct questions: "What do CPAs do?" "What kinds of skills do they have?"

The next part of this process is to translate career skills into personal attributes and experiences. Your choices in course work and extracurricular activities need to take on a sense of purpose. If practical experience is required, then you need to think about an internship or a part-time job. If CPAs spend a lot of time resolving specific problems, then you need Problem Solver skills. As suggested in Chapter 9, take a course in logic or analytical thinking, and begin to group these skills together on your resume.

There is a huge difference between building a resume throughout your college career and simply typing one up during your last semester on campus. It is the difference between marketing and selling. It is also the difference between a Walkman and a widget.

6. Choose Courses Wisely

In many respects, college is a numbers game. At most colleges and universities you can earn a bachelor's degree by taking forty to forty-eight courses. That's five courses each term, or ten to twelve a year, depending on whether your campus is on the quarter or semester system. After four or five years you will accumulate your forty to forty-eight courses and be rewarded with a diploma. If your objective is merely to graduate, the process is simple: Pass the minimum number of courses while "filling in the blanks," that is, taking the necessary distribution, prerequisite, and major classes. On the other hand, if your objective is to learn and to prepare yourself for life and a career in business, your approach should be different, very different.

We recommend that you view each class as an opportunity. You or your family are paying lots of money for this thing called a college education; it's a very big investment. If you added up the costs of tuition, room and board, and books and supplies and divided the total by the total number of class hours, you would see that education has a *direct* cost. At a community college that cost is generally modest; at a small private college the cost runs between $20 and $40 per hour. In essence, after every class hour over a four-year college career (almost a thousand in all), you write your professor a check.

Knowing that the charge is, say, $30 per hour, would anyone sign up for a class based merely on the time of day it is taught? Yet that is exactly what some students do. Would anyone choose a course because the professor doesn't assign any papers? Yet that is what some students do. Would someone take any course indiscriminately, just to fill a requirement? Yet some students do that as well.

We have suggested over twenty-five classes you might consider. Our list includes courses in the arts, philosophy, and sociology, as well as in business. These are taken in addition to major and required general education courses. Remember, you do not have time in college to take courses for the wrong reasons, and the time of day they are offered and lightness of the workload are the wrong reasons.

Even though four years sounds like a long time, it passes very quickly. So choose courses for the right reasons: because you will gain a more multicultural perspective, because you will improve your writing skills, because the professor is interesting and demanding, because you will develop your creativity. A college graduate is not someone who has merely passed the graduation requirements but rather someone who has had the opportunity to learn.

7. Scan the Horizon

Businesses do not exist in a vacuum. Their success or failure is not based solely upon their own actions. One company can make all the right decisions and still go bankrupt, while another can thrive in spite of itself. The unknown and uncontrollable factor is the environment. This environment contains cultural and social elements, economic and technological elements, and political and legal elements. The competition is also part of the larger environment.

Successful companies are those that look *outward* and *forward*. Successful firms avoid the temptation to focus solely on their own business. While understanding that their job is to produce a product or a service, they do not assume an ostrichlike position in their daily affairs. Good management keeps one eye on the business and the other looking outward; the latter provides the company with valuable information on relevant legal cases, new technologies, and social trends, any one of which could put the company out of business or create an exciting opportunity. The adjectives to describe the successful firms of the 1990s are *flexible, fast, street smart,* and *change oriented.* Information is what will drive these firms.

As an individual destined to work well into the twenty-first century, you must also see yourself and act as an information specialist. That sounds good, but the fact remains that most people are lousy scanners. In business, the vast majority of employees concentrate on two short-term goals: getting the job done and solving any problems that arise during the course of doing the job. The job is defined in real time: right now. It involves getting the product or service out the door. What with all the problems on the way to accomplishing that task, it's no wonder little time is left for the wider view.

Similarly, as a student your job is to go to class, study, acquire knowledge, and, of course, get good grades. There are always problems and conflicting demands on your time—exams, term papers, projects. But in addition to meeting those demands, you need to find the time—say, a couple of hours a week—to begin scanning. Begin by developing a reading list. Pick a few magazines, perhaps *Fortune, Forbes,* and *Business Week.* Daily newspapers like the *Wall Street Journal* and the *New York Times* are great sources of information. Make them a habit. Do not use cost as an excuse not to read; the *Wall Street Journal* and virtually all magazines offer attractive discounts to college students.

Let's consider just one example of "scanning." Do you remember the hit 1989 movie *Working Girl?* The young heroine is trying to break out of the secretarial ranks. She gets ideas from scanning lots of different information sources, from the *Wall Street Journal* to the gossip columns of local newspapers. Unlike the more senior and experienced managers around her, the heroine has the ability to connect seemingly unrelated bits of data to create useful information that forms the foundation for key business opportunities.

Scanning will make classroom lectures and textbooks come alive. It's one thing to study the mechanics of a leveraged buyout; it's something else to follow the story of a company going through one, as reported in the *Wall Street Journal, Business Week, Fortune, Forbes,* or other professional publications. A marketing student can learn about the new product development process in class, but reading an in-depth story of a company that turned itself around with a hot new product makes the process real. An article on the political maneuvering behind tax law changes gives a course in tax accounting a more human perspective.

The pace of change is staggering. You need to keep up. You need to stay informed about the world around you. Remember, businesses do not exist in a vacuum. Neither can you.

The Formula for SUCCESS

This book, like most others intended for young people, is filled with advice. Between us we've earned seven degrees, including two Ph.D.'s. (One college degree apiece just was not enough; we kept going back until we did it right!) We have also been college professors, advisers to young people, and consultants to colleges, big corporations, and small businesses. So we think we know a thing or two about college and careers and the transition from sitting in class to sitting in an office after you finish your degree.

Our advice has been fairly comprehensive; we have covered the full spectrum, from classes to computers, from business ethics to business management. We have suggested that you dream and philosophize. We have also identified specific courses and extracurricular activities that can help you develop skills that will be essential in your future career. We have tried to build lighthouses.

The number of facts, figures, examples, and references in this book is substantial. Indeed, we structured the book this way. We intended to share with you a large part of the information we have collected over the years even if, at times, it would be a bit overwhelming. When in doubt, we decided to include it.

But in the final analysis, the best advice is the most obvious, the most straightforward, the simplest. When a young person asked the legendary actor Spencer Tracy for help in his own acting, Tracy gave some valuable advice: "Just learn your lines, and don't bump into the furniture." Tracy was right. It wouldn't make much difference how great an actor the young man was from a technical point of view if he kept forgetting his lines and stumbling all over the furniture.

Aim So High You'll Never Be Bored

*The
greatest waste
of our
natural resources
is the
number of
people
who never
achieve their
potential.
Get out
of that
slow lane.
Shift
into that
fast lane.
If you think
you can't,
you won't.
If you think
you can,
there's a
good chance
you will.
Even making
the effort
will make
you feel
like a new
person.
Reputations
are made
by searching
for things that
can't be done
and doing them.
Aim low:
boring.
Aim high:
soaring.*

In the same sense, it doesn't make any difference how well you carry out the steps to success in the previous pages unless you exhibit one essential personal quality: *the unwillingness to accept any form of mediocrity in yourself.* There is no tool, technique, or training that can overcome a lack of commitment or passion for excellence. Pride is the engine of success. A proud person shuns "just getting by," sees being average as a curse, and has little tolerance for an uninspired effort.

Please understand that your effort is your signature. It says everything about you. So attempt to do your very best at every opportunity in your college career. Each exam, every paper or problem assignment, and every interaction with a professor is an opportunity to shine. It may not translate into an *immediate* job, a higher starting salary, a heated parking space, or a corner office. But it *will* help you develop a healthy mindset, an inspired attitude, a passion for high quality in everything you do. And that effort will have its own ultimate reward.

Success is simple and it is yours for the taking. Indeed, it can be reduced to a formula—SUCCESS: *S*uccess *U*ltimately *C*omes from *C*ommitted *E*ffort and *S*uperior *S*kills. This book is a map for finding the sources of skills enhancement. However, you must provide the effort; you must be committed. Taken together, skills and commitment result in a powerful and winning combination: *a valued college degree and the foundation for a successful business career for the twenty-first century.*

About the Authors

Kenneth C. Green is a senior research associate at the Center for Scholarly Technology at the University of Southern California. Prior to assuming his position at USC in 1989, Dr. Green was associate director of both UCLA's Higher Education Research Institute and the annual American Council on Education/UCLA Cooperative Institutional Research Program, the nation's oldest and largest empirical study of higher education. The author or editor of eight books and some two dozen articles in academic and professional publications, Green has often been quoted on higher education issues in the *Wall Street Journal, New York Times, Los Angeles Times,* and other newspapers and periodicals. Dr. Green lives in Encino, California, with his wife, Rika (a health-care consultant), and two children, Aaron and Mara.

Daniel T. Seymour is a consulting associate for KPMG Peat Marwick, one of the world's largest accounting and management consulting firms. Formerly an associate professor of marketing and assistant to the president at the University of Rhode Island, Dr. Seymour has also taught at the College of William and Mary and has been a visiting scholar at UCLA's Higher Education Research Institute. In addition to his academic experience, Dr. Seymour was also director of marketing for the Bank of New England. He is the author or editor of six books and monographs on marketing, business policy, and higher education issues. An avid scuba diver, Dr. Seymour is also a certified marine research diver. He lives in Los Angeles.

MORE OUTSTANDING TITLES FROM PETERSON'S

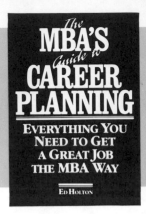

1991 INTERNSHIPS
Over 50,000 On-the-Job Training Opportunities for College Students & Adults
Edited by Brian Rushing

The most complete annual directory available for college students and career-changers seeking on-the-job training positions in any of 23 career fields.

You can't get a job without experience, but you can't get experience without a job. That's why thousands of college students and adults changing careers or re-entering the work force turn to *Internships* every year to find temporary jobs that will open doors to full-time work. The 1991 edition lists over 50,000 positions in 23 career fields (including communications, human services, public affairs, and science/industry), with complete details on the position, desired qualifications, compensation, how to contact, and more.

"An excellent directory for individuals of all ages seeking internships."

—*Better Homes & Gardens*

$27.95 paperback

THE MBA'S GUIDE TO CAREER PLANNING
Ed Holton

This is the most practical and thorough book yet published for current and prospective business graduate students. Using a proven system for MBA career planning, it shows how to gain the edge in the job search process and addresses the special concerns of MBAs as only an "insider" can do, helping MBAs to:

- Assess their interests and abilities
- Market themselves effectively
- Negotiate job offers

Here is a storehouse of helpful perspectives and insights, such as:

- The realities of the job market
- What to know about an employer
- Assessing corporate culture

The book's appendix is a detailed listing of important publications on the popular MBA concentrations, including finance, marketing, manufacturing, consulting, and advertising.

The author: Ed Holton is director of the MBA Program at Virginia Polytechnic Institute and State University.

"Give the book fifteen minutes. . . . You won't be able to put it down."

—Anthony T. Cobb
Associate Professor of Management
Virginia Polytechnic Institute
and State University

$16.95 paperback